C000204729

GOD'S LONELY MEN
(WORD IS SAVING GOD'S LONELY MEN)

PETE HAYNES

HEADHUNTER BOOKS
www.headhunterbooks.co.uk

First published in November 2007 by Head-Hunter Books

ISBN 978-1-906085-04-9

Head-Hunter Books
www.headhunterbooks.co.uk
www.myspace.com/headhunterbooks

Printed by Butler and Tanner

CONTENTS

For Ma and Pa.
&
For those about whom I care –
some have skin and some fur or hair.
Some walk upright with painted nails –
and some on all fours with sticky out tails.

Acknowledgements

Cover artwork: Billy Forward.

Thanks to:
The other members of The Lurkers,
M. Brewer,
P. Edwards,
M. (T-shirt) Flatman,
L. Heggarty,
P. Kelly,
J. King,
M. King,
Max and the Fulham Crowd,
Neil (Ug) the roadie,
M. Stone,
M. Wyeth,

&

the people who helped and supported The Lurkers.

Foreword

I went to school in Northwest London and, in my early teens, was right into David Bowie and his music. Then along came the sound of punk which freshened up the whole music scene. Out went the dinosaurs of rock like Led Zeppelin and Deep Purple who, at the time, were doing those huge stadium tours. Pubs, clubs and small venues then slung open their doors and the ordinary kids from the streets got up on stage and played. It was a breath of fresh air. I was 14 or 15 at the time and the whole attitude of the scene drew me in. Me and a few mates even took to taking bog chains and sink plugs and wore them around our necks. The Stranglers were one of my favourite bands but the Sex Pistols, The Clash, The Ruts, Stiff Little Fingers and, of cause, the Lurkers blared from my bedroom stereo. I was even on the Lurkers, Gods Lonely Men, album cover. If you look closely you can see me and a mate in the crowd at one of their gigs at the Marquee Club in London.

I once went out wearing pyjamas with screen printing on the back; just how the Boomtown Rats had dressed when they appeared on Top of The Pops. New wave music definitely left a mark on my life, I loved the feel of the whole thing; the people, the music, the clothes. The punk scene had such a huge influence on fashion and music not just in the 70's but even today. Music up until Punk arrived had stagnated and nothing had changed for 25 years, then bang, young kids with lots to say and bundles of energy were up there on stage full of anger and frustration playing high speed Rock and Roll with lyrics we could associate with and understand. Besides the odd bit of spitting and pushing and shoving and pogo-ing in time to the music, there was no real trouble at gigs.

When I became a professional footballer, I'd take my music into the dressing room before and after a game. I remember being at Nottingham Forest and we'd have The Clash or The Stranglers coming out of the speakers. Both Brian Clough and Frank Clarke would throw some strange looks in my direction at my choice of music. One time, I even borrowed the club mini-bus off of the Forest groundsman and took a few of the boys to a Punk gig up at Leeds.

Even now I still listen to New Wave and Punk along with today's bands like Green Day, Marilyn Manson and The Stereophonics who all have that punk influence in the sound of their music. 80's bands like U2 and Nirvana came along after that initial 70's burst and went on to become huge bands.

As time has gone by over the years, I've personally met quite a few of the bands I used to look up to and go and watch. I've met The Lurkers and The Stranglers and they're real nice people. I've been going to the annual Wasted Festival for the last 5 or 6 years which is a big Punk festival that seems to get bigger every year. I left school in 1978 and went to gigs all over London and still now I love going to see live bands. You can't beat it. I grew up with the sound of punk and the passion for it has never left me. It played a massive part in mine and many people's lives. I still listen to it as I drive to work. I've got The Ruts CD in the car stereo as I write this, Babylon's Burning they sing as the music thumps out. White Riot and London's Burning sang The Clash which were classics and will stand the test of time. Just like Punk music itself, it's timeless.

Stuart Pearce, MBE.
Manager of the England Under 21's

2007

Introduction

In 'God's Lonely Men', Pete Haynes takes us on an insider's journey through the late seventies Punk Rock phenomenon whilst maintaining an outsider's view on society at large from his position as the drummer in West London hopefuls 'The Lurkers'. Pete charts their progress from the pubs and clubs to Top of the Pops and back again, giving us a wry look at the music business in the process. But this is much more than a 'warts 'n all' look at the rock 'n' roll industry; here we see future rock stars soon to have the world at their feet, rubbing shoulders with everyday people struggling against the odds to find their feet in the world.

It is a story that mixes brutal humour with a sharp critique of the human condition from the point of view of a working class individual who, despite often being at odds with the world around him, still finds a connection with like minded souls along the way.

More than a mere rock 'n' roll fable, 'God's Lonely Men' is for anyone interested in 'people' and their attitudes towards one another in a tale which looks at right and wrong and is never afraid to take sides.

L.H.

Un

They don't call me Manic for nothing. I have written down my story and would like to dedicate it to all sentient beings; even humans.

For me and for many others, 'Punk Rock' gave an identity and seemed, often very wrongly, to give an answer to the things I felt was going on around that time.

It was ironic and a coincidence how the Radio One DJ Dave Lee Travis figured in my 'punk journey'. One afternoon whilst at home, I was eighteen or nineteen years old at the time, I was listening to the radio with all the usual stuff and nonsense coming from it, when Dave Lee Travis said in a deep, cosy, greedy voice, I can't quote word for word but he said something like, 'If you have just come home from the office, sit back, kick off your shoes and listen to the smooth sounds of Demis Roussos. 'Pour your lady a glass of wine', etcetera, et-fucking cetera. I was up out of my chair and turned the thing off and didn't listen to the radio for a while to come. I wasn't missing much.

For me, in the main, DJ's sounded staid, middle class men with a bullying attitude who support hunting and have aspirations of being laird of the manor. I saw and see a lot of them as being clever dick teacher types, arrogant and piss taking if you're not marching in step with the rest of the army. I am sure there are loads of eighteen or nineteen year olds that think the same now; I hope ! I suppose a way of combating this feeling was to strike back. Not to throw a Molotov cocktail. I wouldn't have known what one of them was at that time and definitely would have put my money on it being something you drink that didn't come in a pint glass. No, like many others, I wanted to channel that anger and aggression at the unfairness of it all into music. For me and I shared this feeling with The Lurkers' guitarist Pete Stride throughout, I felt that I had a feeling of confusion and, when younger, feeling I had more in common with a person from a Day Centre for people with a mental disability than being part of a scene. To often feel an internal torture and at times to escape by deriving pleasure from something naive, one of life's very simple pleasures, yet something that was mine; the feeling of being powerless is dealt with in this way. Yes, at odds with one's environment but how to challenge this cold and distant society ?

With music ?

I had an empathy with (and that I could relate to more) the scared distorted figure in the shadow rather than belong to a placard waving student culture.

The Lurkers were John Steinbeck rather than Trotsky; the importance was to convey the meaning of sentimentalism, the subjectivity of the 'little person' rather than political alienation in the grand scheme. Our characters would not rejoice at revolution for social change as they feel they do not belong or would not be invited with the 'mass'. They do not share the same principles. I am talking of people who are socially aside, personally disfigured and fractured: 'it's quiet here'.

To be a rebel ?
I didn't know what a rebel was.

People told me that was what I did, rebel - but I wasn't conscious of it.
I was thrown out of school at fourteen years of age; the leaving age was fifteen then. I didn't go to another school, none of the local schools wanted me. Good. The place had deceitful bullying teachers who engaged in sexual practices that eventually caused three of them to take their own lives. It was one of the last schools in the South East of England to have a boxing ring set up but it was used to satisfy the urges of a couple of teachers who would make boys fight it out. When it was obvious that one the boys didn't want to fight because he was being bullied in the first place and this 'teacher' comes along and throws him in the ring and so he gets beaten up again but this time within the rules. When a boy would point out to the teacher that it wasn't fair because one the boys in the ring didn't want to fight and it was obvious because he was standing there with one knee raised and his arms around his face in an effort to protect himself and crying out for it all to stop, the teacher would offer the boy who had objected to the spectacle to get in the ring with him.

There, boys who came from a nearby orphanage that went to the school wore any colour blazer they were given but usually not the colour of Abbotsfield. This made the boys stand out yet the only bullying they suffered, that I saw, came from the snivelling and cowardly 'teachers'.

The school was useless. It was a post war experiment built between three large estates. My mum was told by one of the teachers that he fully expected me to spend most of my life in prison and that's rich coming from a bunch of men who were most probably walking around with their dicks caught in mousetraps and stuffed up their arses. The place taught the boys that disgusting and deceitful people run the world.

However, I never felt I was rebelling against anything. In fact I always thought I would be that man in the smart suit, smoking a Peter Stuyvesant, striding purposefully into one of those glass office blocks, the symbolism of power and progression in the late 1960's and early 1970's and nodding at the secretaries and the other 'guys' at work as I entered this concrete and glass colossus.

Why ? How could this come about ? To be '*normal*' ?

When the foundation had been set for a course away from the dominant babble in our society, I wasn't aware of it. Was I living in a dream ? Maybe. 'Upstairs' I can be King, out here I queue for bread.

To rebel against one's 'parents' ? I didn't understand it; my dad did not have a position in society to rebel against. He is one of twelve or fourteen who lived in half a house just off the Wandsworth Bridge Road in Fulham, very poor. He went all the way through the Second World War and then did labouring work, begrudgingly. Like many others, Dad was too sensitive for his environment. He lost himself listening to 'cowboy' music, never drank, lived in the same council house since the war and still does.

My mum came from a tiny community in South Wales. Having to leave school at thirteen, she went into service as a maid in some place she refers to as the 'castle'. They were good enough to give her one Wednesday afternoon off a month and paid her the equivalent of twelve and a half pence a week. It ingrained servility into a naturally very kind and humble person. Mum was seventeen when war broke out. She went to Swansea and worked in a sort of makeshift hospital that was an old workhouse. Some of the old patients/residents were injured servicemen from the previous war. Poor bastards. Most of them were mad or worse and discarded by people sharing the same blood. She has had a hard life. Like many others, she is meek and sees the view of the 'underdog'.

Rebel against them ? No. Feel angry at the 'system' ? Yes.

I would hear some young people talk of their "Father's drinks' cabinet" and talk of their parents as if they were from a different sphere and I was to discover that "father's" manner, position and possessions were really to be looked up to and to be learned by and sometimes despised. It wasn't my experience. Coming from a predominately middle class area with all its petty snobbery and realising the frustrating fact that there are those who judge and are prejudiced against a child because he or she comes from a certain type of house and not seeing the talent or merit in a person did leave scars and you learn about the British class system at an early age.

As a youngster I knew fuck all about the 'system', about how it was organised or the slots and opportunities it afforded. I saw work from my dad's perspective; begrudgingly giving one's time to do boring low paid repetitive work/labour in repressive conditions and having relationships with people at work based on fear and suspicion. Dad always played 'Make The World Go Away' by Jim Reeves at home when things got on top of him. Exactly.

My experiences in later life of being condemned by the arty social worker types as a 'thug', NFer type because of being on the stocky side, liking a drink and having a West London accent has, and I would be lying to deny it, pissed me off. Having sensitivity or an enquiring mind to the way things are presented to us can often be negated by those in the middle class who are in favour of stereotyping people in order to control them. It is often presented that to come from a certain social economic background like 'working class' means that you lean and aspire to holidays in Spain, what 'motor' is driven, chunky jewellery, singing "I'm forever blowing bubbles", have the biggest satellite dish in the street, having a family 'get together' with a knees ups, disliking people because of the colour of their skin and accusing anyone with a lisp of being a queer etc, etc, et-fucking etc.

No, to be at odds with basic conditioning, can, if you are not thick skinned, shuttle you off to the margins and maybe worse.

I have shared these feelings with Arturo, my friend for many years. He experienced many fears as a child on the estate where he came from, of feeling scared and anxiously worrying over concerns of his family. To be nervous and have a feeling of being different, enforced daily by bullying for not having 'the' football kit or adhering to the values and behaviour and then in later life a feeling of not fitting in with whatever 'social band' you tune into.

Some people grow up to hurt others for the way they feel, some hurt themselves, some explode in knee jerk physical violence and there are those who internalise emotions that disturb for years.

I was seen by the 'system' as a yob but I did not feel as if I was and wasn't seen as one by my peers. I wasn't settled and saw myself as introverted. This was not conveyed externally and I was often seen as 'the mad person'.

About his time, for around a year, I went to this club called Ickenham Hall. I wasn't involved as a known participating member and was often banned for not complying with the rules but at fifteen I could have strayed and I am sure that goes for some of the other boys who went to this rather strange little club. It wasn't run by the formal social worker type, abreast with the contemporary fad politics of the time; it was in fact eccentric. It was run by an old lady called Mrs Bevan. She was about four feet eleven and looked much smaller because she had a damaged spine which caused her to lean right back as she walked. Her long suffering husband was in attendance every evening. These two were out of kilter with the social service system and eventually the place withered and changed as the old couple were moved out the way by the 'caring professionals' who have created a self-perpetuating industry for themselves and, needless to say, the club that offered something for young people does not now exist.

I think 'eccentric' is the right word for describing quite a few of the characters around my area. It can be seen as a sort of protected enclosure and giving rise to a particular personality. Mrs Bevan was a good character and, I believe, a good person. She knew that a lot of the youngsters going there were a little on the misfit side and some were representatives of the official misfit groups such as the visiting Hells Angels that used to roar up to this leafy little club. There were members of the Windsor Chapter, Road Rats and the local Nomads. I had a skinhead haircut, Harrington jacket (pink !), braces and boots but hung around for a while with some of these chaps. A few had come out of prison and I remember one bloke, his name was 'Ape', a shaven headed very powerfully built Hells Angel being reprimanded by Mrs Bevan on the steps of the club for some matter. I can't remember what it was but I can remember her voice and the tone of it. "Ape, now listen to me, this is not good enough," she admonished him in her very correct English. It painted a funny and weird scene. I reckon those Angels had the utmost respect for this woman. In my experience, honesty goes a long way and is understood especially by those who see through and can't accept the double dying bollocks.

I believe the club was good for me. I broadened, mixing with grammar school types having their different ways and I was influenced by some of the people I met. Whilst at school where there was no discipline or respect, at the hall it was different. Mrs Bevan made me show an interest in one of the structured activities. There was drama, pottery, archery, along with other pursuits, giving an experience not had at school.

The club was close to my house on our side of the bridge. Ickenham was and is to a lesser extent, divided by the railway track and the railway bridge was its version of a checkpoint. The 'other side' was the posh side having the petty snobbery. My mum worked in a grocery shop when I was a child and she told of the terrible snobby manner and artificial posturing of some of the people, mostly the blue rinse brigade. As mum said, 'they wanted their cheese sliced so thin you could read the paper through it but they made no mistake in ordering a thicker slice on double stamp day.

Yes, the hang 'em high neurotics from bigot county. I will always remember the local library where the various newspapers were on show in a little rack with a polite notice under them reading, 'The Daily Mail is kept at the counter'. Those evil little shopping baskets could not possibly be carrying orrf The Mail by mistake; surely not ?

An incident that happened to me when I was about eleven was similar to one experienced by my brother Dave when he was about nine. I was invited around to this boy's house on the other side of the bridge. His mum, coming forth with all snot but no cup of tea asked her son to go into the kitchen where I heard her ask him where I lived. On telling the old bag, I heard her strained rattle of a voice order that I be asked to leave. Pleasant.

The club was predominately made up of youngsters coming from the 'other side' and many of them were very good to me. But, as I say, I didn't go there for long, yet I feel its influence on me was a good one. I did labouring work in a local junkyard before becoming the age of fifteen to start proper work. When I bunked off from school I used to go to June's Café. It was a haunt for youngsters, some Hells Angels and some others being serious pinball players. I remember on one occasion a biker rode his bike through the doors of the cafe and right up to the counter and then ordered a cup of tea. Funny enough, a bunch of American youngsters connected with the nearby American air base had formed a group. They were called America and had a famous single called A Horse With No Name. A couple of the bikers I used to speak to worked part time in the junkyard that was close by. They told me that there was a job going in the yard. I went and saw the owner and he gave me the once over and told me that he'd give me a start. A couple of the chaps that worked there were gypsies. They were day labourers usually spending their money in a pub at night, often getting in scrapes and not being the most reliable for the boss. However, they were very pleasant to me. We used to go in the pub at lunchtime and I would have a brown and mild. There was a certain type of dishonest honesty about that scrap game and when I entered the world of the *normals*, I realised, like a lot of young people do, that most adults in the world of work are sneaky and crawling and an honest request can be dealt with as a weakness.

A few jobs rocketed by in the first year at work. The quickest being two and a half hours working in a modern day sweatshop where they nailed pallets together, some having 'Coca Cola' burned into the sides of them. I threatened the foreman, swearing at him after he repeatedly made criticisms of my standard of work. At sixteen I worked for a building company as a labourer, concrete laying, unloading lorries that kind of stuff. We were building a crematorium onto an existing crematorium, a new chapel, ovens, the lot. I should never have worked there. In winter, some of us used to go into the oven room to have our sandwiches and tea, it being warm in there as four gas ovens would be burning bodies. One of the blokes that worked there used to show me how to rake the body around. The bones and ashes would go into this tumble dryer affair having iron balls to crush them into dust. Then, they would put the remaining dust into a plastic bag. It would then be spread onto the gardens or collected by relatives or whatever.

I don't know why, I wasn't making a point or anything, maybe it was because I was just a tight sod but I took a load of these plastic bags that they used to put the ashes in. New ones that is. My mum would put my sandwiches in them. This was seen by the old Irish labourers as something terrible as if my Marmite sandwiches were taking the place of a transient spirit and something diabolical and curse-like will surely befall me. Maybe they were right.

The old labourers would ask me to clean their shovels and hods for them in a water butt that was directly beneath the chimney of the crem'. I thought nothing of this but I used to remark about this thick greasy layer of murky translucent slime that I would peel from the top of the water before washing out the tools. One day, an old Irish man, his face cringing, said to me, "It doesn't bother you none, then, son ?" Nodding at the greasy substance I was peeling off and throwing onto the ground. "Nah," I said. They must have thought I was some kind of devil worshipping heathen or whatever. He turned to his friend and said, "He doesn't feel the need to cover his hands and his mother packs his sandwiches in the bags they put the bodies in." His friend tutted and they both shook their heads at the blasphemy of it all. Even my mum was brought in as part of the Godless, guiltless or whatever. I didn't realise that the greasy slime was in fact human skin, formed by a collection of drifting particles from the chimney. As I say, I should never have worked there. The images of the burning bodies have stayed with me and, at that age, having no direction was bad enough but being there with some of the miserable bastards working around the place wasn't good at all. Yet, some valuable experiences and lessons can arise from any situation.

Some mornings, early, a van would arrive that was unmarked carrying the dead body of an unknown person, someone found dead in a ditch or railway embankment, someone alone with nobody to organise the details of death. One winter's morning, I asked an old fellow who had worked there for years about this whilst watching a grey van drive silently away after dropping off the body of a dead person. He told me that the circumstances are investigated. They are usually tramps that died by themselves, their only company being loneliness, madness and drink. 'God's Lonely Men'. This man told me that, when the council delivered a body, the crematorium would contact the major religions to see if a representative of that particular brand would like to say an official farewell, as it were. He told me that in the years he had worked there not one person from one of the religions had taken up the invitation. Now, I didn't know much about organised religion but I was learning an awful lot about hypocrisy. My education was not formal. I was insecure and, not having much guidance from home, I felt shared feelings with the 'weak' and it felt, as it still does, incredibly cruel to see the irreverence and indifference shown to those who fall or do not come up to measure. But, death is a great leveller as they say and there was a particular incident that cheered me greatly.

The body of a lone man had arrived one morning. His unmarked coffin was put on one side to be burned before the daily schedule, then had to be bagged and spread on the gardens as was the usual practice. Anyway, this same day the body of some 'important' dignitary to do with the military or some such pomp was to be cremated. A family representative had given the men in the oven room an ornate personalised silver urn. The plan was for a ceremony to take place. A marching band with family and military colours gathered in the car park, all witnessed by titles, hangers on and the press. The ashes of the Duke, Earl or whoever was to be put in this silver urn having the family crest on it. The urn was then taken to the family home where it was to be placed in a reserved spot on the mantelpiece or the cultural equivalent and took its place amongst other family bits and pieces. Well, the two men working in the oven room named the tramp, who had arrived that morning, as 'Fred'. One of them called me to one side and told me that it's good to get even in life when you can. He had kept Fred's ashes to one side, burned the body of the titled man and put his ashes in the plastic bag that was sprinkled out on the gardens and Fred's were put in the silver urn. The band finished, the hymns stopped and they all went off carrying with them the ashes of an unknown man called 'Fred' in the revered silver urn. So, there it is to this day I suppose, being introduced to and saluted to by a bunch of sycophantic wankers.

Whilst working at the crematorium I bought a drum kit from Chas, a friend of mine. The drums had apparently been owned by the drummer in the sixties group Unit Four Plus Two. This was not an actual selling point but it remained a significant talking point when I spoke to people about 'where I got them'. Matters like this have no interest whatsoever to anyone having a flicker of a life of their own but there you are. The boring inanity of people in groups and those that follow them knows no bounds. It does not matter what it is or how tenuous a connection there might be, if it can be related to music in some way, there are people that will share that particular minority interest with others also having an esoteric knowledge of that particular thing and it can be a talking point for hours, months or even years. Things like going to the town where a specific drum fitting is made, swapping stubs of entry tickets to gigs, visiting a pub where a group might have met before they became famous or the different types of polish used when making a guitar. Do you see what I mean ?

This was not the first time I had an interest in the drums. When I was about nine or ten my brother, who is three years older than me, was taken a few times to see The Who rehearse at the Young Vic. Dave was a big fan of The Who and other pop music and my mum used to speak to the mothers of two of The Who's roadies who lived nearby. They arranged for Dave to see them rehearse on Sunday afternoons. At home, I used to bang along on the seat of a chair to 'I'm A Boy' and 'Happy Jack'. Dave told Keith Moon this who very kindly took time to speak to Dave and gave him a bunch of drumsticks for me to hold when whacking the chair. Unfortunately, I broke the sticks although I have managed to save one of them as a keepsake.

My other experience of playing the drums at an early age was when I was about the age of eight, having bought a tin drum in a jumble sale for about the equivalent of under one pence and formed a group with my school friend Ray Brown. He bought a blue plastic Beatles guitar for half a crown and the two of us formed a group which we gave an original name - 'The Dave Clark Two', playing no more than about three times and only in Ray's dad's garage.

Anyway, back to buying my drum kit. I would get on the bus to see this man who lived in Hayes. He was a bit of a light jazz/cocktail drummer I suppose,

a typically English sort of jazzy bloke from that generation. I was interested in
Keith Moon and he would make me play with brushes to 'Raindrops Keep
Falling On My Head' having to hold the brushes in the military style with a
cushion under my left arm for discipline and style. I was not hip and nor was he.
I have always liked the sound of a jazzy swing drummer but this was not hitting
home. I went to another jazz drummer who also lived in Hayes but it all seemed
like learning maths or something; two or three lessons and he realised that I was
not an 'A - Grade student'.

During this time I worked as a builder's labourer for companies and individuals,
then doing a few dead end jobs in warehouses and the like before getting a job
in an Esso petrol station in Hayes End when I was nineteen or twenty. From the
age of fifteen, I had developed a habit of using pubs for a social life. Drinking
heavily at seventeen, I decided that I was going to give up drinking gin. It was
always loads of beer and lots of 'shorts' to follow. My propensity to find things
interesting that many might find stupid or dangerous has often led me to gain
company and insights with the estranged and gain insights into the mind on
the periphery. Although Ickenham is a small suburban area, I believe it is a
place having more than its fair share of oddness. When I was about nineteen,
often drunk, I would be cornered by a character that would rant politics at me.
Then, following this up, he would knock on my door on a Sunday morning. I
used stand there in the hallway, suffering with a hangover, whilst he showed me
magazines from the far right, such as Klu Klux Clan material having cartoons
intended to be satirical which were as subtle as a concept called 'London Brick
Company' smashing you in the face. "Morning," he would say to my mum, "just
showing your son here the truth." Some people have the Jehovah Witnesses.
Not long afterwards he was arrested having a drink in a pub down the end of
my road with a senior member of the KKK. It made the Sunday papers and
the KKK man later went on to be a Republican politician in the United States
of America.

However, although I did not make a conscious study of the misfit, I always
seemed to end up in the company of the lonely people who are often called
'nutters'. Caricatures of this type of person are often portrayed in television
comedy and the people that I'm talking about have nothing to do with the
BBC's type of acceptable eccentric where they celebrate an individual who
wears odd socks, a large bow tie and pulls mad facial expressions. Sometimes
his life is slotted in on the tail end of a local news programme, sleeping for one
night in the shed dressed as a kipper and drinks his morning cup of tea from
a shoe which belongs to his boss; and all for charity. It then often turns out
that Mr Strangeperson is a Headmaster and he describes his children as gifted

and intelligent, one of each, one doing languages, the other the piano. His wife walked around Upper Volta for the local Guide group, picking that destination because she knew that her peers/competitors would not know where it was and 'aren't they just the most *amazing* family ?' See ? They are not 'nutters' at all. They are safe.

No, it's not that kind of thing at all. At one time I found it interesting to carry a small yellow rubber ring, a little large for my pocket but I would take it out with me at nights and show it to people I hadn't met before. I wasn't intentionally trying to shock people or looking for a response but maybe I was, although it certainly was not conventional teenage rebellion. It had stuck in my mind and made an impression when one of these older solitary men, who I usually met in dusty old public bars, had shown me something simple and in a way bizarre. Maybe it was just an old watch or an unbelievable photograph of them or their family from many years before; for me it was not just stupid, a meaningless moment, to be seen as a person and action to be discarded. I magnified it. I suppose seeing it as a symbol, it represented more than just, say, a broken shoehorn. I knew that I had sometimes been referred to as 'the mad person' and it was this imagery, this voice of the mad that my sympathies lay with in searching for the truth.

George Orwell's character in Nineteen Eighty Four sought the company of the 'prols' for information. I leant towards the company of the lonely, the mad people, out of step, often despised and thrown out of pubs, jeered and laughed at, persecuted and lied about, blamed and through the course of our history serving a function for scapegoating as the *normals* cannot accept responsibility for the inexplicable in human behaviour with all its atrocities. No, we cannot accept it as being the actions of sane humans; rather we put the blame on animals or the actions of mad people. So, a life for many is to occupy a marginal existence, being condemned and brought in as a cause or for a reason why there are grotesque ruptures in our social and psychological fabric. And yet, from their position of being aside, maybe a clearer observation can be made of the rushing, twisting, changing and hurtling along nature in our fragile course which is our 'being'. Maybe I was on a course to search for the truth, maybe it is in that speck of paint that the disgruntled mad artist had discarded, it could be there, apart and different. I was seeing the fool as honest, not affected by a self-limiting cocoon maintained by fear and ignorance.

It is as if we self-police ourselves, a self-slavery, our potentials never realised, our compassion never expressed as the repressing fear takes us away from sharing our self with others, yet aside from ourselves.

Why was it when studying models of power with its arrogance and dominance, it was not to corporations or governments that I sighted my gaze but rather at the person, those interactions on the small scale ? It was with people's treatment of those who appear different, those seen as weaker or vulnerable; it was through those actions I felt I witnessed the nucleus to a process of self-hate that maybe will be our downfall. And people's futile expenditure of energy is wasted on suppressed wanting, yearning and expectations and resentments are aimed at those who are blamed for eluding us of that elusive self we feel that we should be rewarded with but this thing is blocking us from attaining this self and so there is a feeling of being denied. And I felt that maybe it was within the actions of those that are different that I might find my truth. With those very people with their behaviours that we the *normals* are taught to judge ourselves by and against in the process of self maintenance in order to create an identity that fits and belongs with others but not with 'The Other'. The 'other', I saw them and identified with them; this unromantic, non-competitive, non-confrontational and certainly not the glamorous savage. No, it was the idiot, the nuisance, the person who is 'in the way'.

In the way of what?

And then, I wanted to pull out a gun and kill somebody. Is that what I thought I was doing with my drum kit ? My metaphorical gun ? I talked about this to Pete Stride. We could form a group that will pronounce 'You don't like us', 'We are not like you', 'Blame us for what is wrong in your life'.

It was this feeling that Pete and I took around publishers and companies, one being Miles Copeland, brother of Stuart, the drummer in The Police. When going around these offices and seeing looks of indifference and dislike on the faces of the people employed in these places in some way strengthened our belief and it felt good. Pete wrote songs like 'Freakshow' and 'Shadow'. I knew that Pete understood. Here I had a medium but not only to use and associate with but also to hide behind.

I started to socialise with Pete Stride when I was about seventeen or eighteen down one of the local pubs; I called him 'Stride' because of his tall height and thus long step when walking. This was not my first meeting with Pete. I had played football against him on one of the greens when we were about thirteen. He was a striker, I was a goalie - it was only jumpers as goal posts stuff.

After my school years, it wasn't youth clubs, football training and girls but labouring work, often having a doomed and looming sense of persecution, ignorance of the society in which I lived and not having an identity that I saw as being me. Maybe like other young people I felt that I was going through a dreamlike existence. My consciousness often caused me to be sad, wrought with anxiety and to have that feeling of being odd and different. Having done fuck all academically at school, I started to read George Orwell, John Steinbeck and then, a little later, books on the fringe of philosophy. A chap called Tony McKee opened my eyes in this area. We decided that we were going to get a group together that wasn't a commercial concept, this was just before the punk fashion. It was based on swing jazz. Neither of us could really play to a standard that would be acceptable but anyway, we wanted people to join the group who were very 'English', gimpy looking types. We planned to have a wrestling scene with body-builders on stage, even boxers hitting bags and attacking the audience, starting fights and returning on stage to play Be Bop jazz with a ranting body-builder *cum* wrestling promoter fused in the scene.

We never played a gig, of course but we did book ourselves with this bass player at a youth *cum* culture centre run by two-faced, boring hippy types for boring bastards with drug problems going there for counselling, coffee and to generally bore the fuck out of each other, knowing all the while that they are all settling for second best and none of them wanted to be in each other's company anyway. Well, that's my opinion. I never spent any time there but I knew of such places. I suppose that is where young people who are having difficulties turn to but I was not on that course. It didn't make sense and I wasn't comfortable with it all. Maybe I hadn't reached the stage of being a 'young person' and I didn't like the so-called professionals that are involved in that industry. As it happened this bass player did not turn up, nor did Tony bloody Mckee. Just me stuck there with a bunch of hippy type, trainee social worker people.

Tony was a drinking friend of Pete (Stride). I was getting to know them but I was also a bit of a loner, going up the West End by myself at weekends and standing in the local pubs during the week. During this time I had the odd menial short termed job. It was through Tony that I gained an interest in the writing of people like Jack Kerouac. I suppose he was aping a studenty type of experience, we lived with our mums and dads, not sharing a studenty, young person's culture but rather bigotry in the suburbs. The music I listened to with Tony was a jazzy kind of thing but always having a connection with boxing. I remember the two of us going to this *arty* cinema up town and seeing "The Jack Johnson Story", the first black heavy weight champion of the world. It had a 1950's Be Bop soundtrack. There was hardly anyone in the cinema. I think Tony wanted to try out a right hook that he had been practising at his boxing club on one the posy, arty types. Marriage and children was soon to fill his life and extinguish his confused aspirations and self imagery of being a jazz bass playing boxing champion who has his opinion asked on political world events; but so it goes, as they say.

My brother's influence on me of liking the old pop music of The Who, Move, Beatles, Kinks, was then later added with The Beachboys, Alice Cooper, Lou Reed, the Velvet Underground and the New York Dolls. So, there we were, a little group of us having tastes away from the *norm* and existing in a place having narrow cultural boundaries. Although Pete did dress in a style that would sometimes bring him ridicule, I was devoid when it came to having a fashionable appearance. At this time Pete used to go up town with Howard Wall, Pete Edwards (Plug) and my brother Dave. Pete Edwards and Howard were school friends of Dave. They used to see some of the groups on the pub rock circuit like The 1 0 1 ers, Dr Feelgood but, whenever they could, The New York Dolls. I didn't bother but all the same, Pete asked me to come round to his home to rehearse with Tony and himself. So, I took a snare drum and cymbal 'over the bridge' to Pete's mum and dad's bungalow and there in that quiet and sedately neurotic suburban road got down to making a racket; a familiar tale in many similar roads throughout this green and pleasant land.

Pete showed me a miniature tambourine; it was pink and made out of plastic. He told me that he had got it at a Marc Bolan concert. Pete tried to impress upon me that Marc had chosen him when he threw out the tambourines to the crowd, throwing this one just for him. In Pete's room were posters of music people, Mick Ronson I remember as being one of them. I never had any posters, photos or anything signifying an identity. Living in a room with two older brothers did not afford the space but I suppose I never developed to having the role model, admiration thing. But, all the same, there we were, talking about the New York Dolls, the meaning of their 'Frankenstein', our shared feeling of an undercurrent of persecution, being the *other*, and then we got down to practice.

Before we got down to rehearse, a ritual would take place which at first I found mad, bizarre or whatever. Pete would carefully place a linen cloth no larger than an handkerchief over the cage where his gerbil lived; this being to protect the little fella's ears as Pete turned up the guitar which sounded like a juggernaut crashing into a chest clinic. It was a wall of sound. I couldn't really play, playing just the 'one beat' for all occasions. That's what I called it. It was a sort of train rhythm played as hard as I could. We practised 'Sweet Jane' which I doubt very much sounded remotely like the song with my one beat and Pete's style which was 'noise'. After the fury and our anger had been released, Pete would, genteelly and with great care, take the hanky sized cloth from the gerbil's cage whispering words of greeting. Strange, I thought, the window frames shook, I had lost the ability to hear or even taste but furry friend seemed unscathed by this suburban ceremony. The gerbil lived an inordinately long life, I am glad to say, as did Pete's cats.

I suppose it was around 1975 and Pete and I had not ventured to a rehearsal studio because we didn't feel comfortable going to a normal place to rehearse. We felt threatened, mind, we felt threatened almost anywhere. Dominant culture wasn't that much different then but, nowadays, there is this post modernist eclectic mix and match of fashion and taste where there is chain store grunge for the aspiring professional at the weekend, a culture of credit card rock and 'controversies' can be about whether you go to Macdonald's or Burger King. I was not into the disco, or as it's now called club, thing. I went about twice. For one thing, I did not have a pair of trousers but the main reason was the repression dripping out of the feared experience; of going to a place with someone at the door searching you, dressed in the ridiculous suit thing. And where young men go in their clean shirts, costing about three days wages, only to be ruined in the conflictual confrontations fuelled by booze, sex and boredom. A feeling of inadequacy is played out to mechanical music, ironically called soul, where all potential of sensitivity is alienated from the soul in the pursuit for mating in an all too often violent exercise. Having no humour or humility, just a basic slapstick, them and us ritual and a winners and losers regime.

The 'prog rock' fashion bored me as I am sure it did many others. This segment of our society's offering for a young man left me cold. I only went to a couple of the gigs and always felt like an undercover policeman and felt that I would be spotted, feeling very uncomfortable. There were the folk rock, best bitter brigade and its followers of dreary sods going on about the kingdom of King Boring Billy meeting the wizard of Whipsnade in a cloud of pink dreams. Then everyone had to discuss it all and write a thesis about it afterwards, speaking in a dull monotone.

Arrgh

As now, British society has its popular culture pretty well sown up by the university types following the lineage of their parents' positions in our society, being involved in comedy, music, journalistic fickledom, media and advertising. Often having a liberal face but concealing behind their backs a sharp weapon to be used for the protection of the status quo, their position in it and thus their power. I went along once or twice to these student union affairs that had gigs with people sitting cross-legged on the floor. Wherever you went, these silly fuckers would plonk right down on the floor in a little group, even if there were a few chairs around. I saw this as them performing some kind of rebellion against the conformity of their parents' 'living' home. The music was academic. Having post gig appraisals as the music was discussed in terms of 'musicianship' and 'intelligence', brimming with the neurotic snobbery that their parents probably had, they were on course to take their place. The only difference being that they were dressed in a different thread.

Of course, the United States' influence in this country is evident, grown nowadays to a near world standardisation of culture. The way I saw it then was as a mid Atlantic mouthwash with the denim invasion having the sounds of Clapton and Skynyrd, films like Easy Rider being sold as a cultural rebellion against the likes of Bing Crosby and the 'straights', only for these sound smiths emanating from the counter culture to readily join the same golf clubs as those they were putting that all-American, 'spin on this', finger up to. The jean-shirted and pony-tailed movement into the media has developed into the new elite, taking as a cultural reference a cool stadium rock democratic appearance, owning large companies, dressed like something out of The Eagles and having a hippy acknowledgement in the tone of the voice but a corporate meaning to the words. For the Bransons with their happy smiley companies, there are no unions allowed. Akin to a kind of Victorian philanthropist, altruistic comments backed with acts of charity. A trick I have always thought they learned from methods of subduing the poor in places like India and how these people flourished under the monetarist reign that ruled this country in the 1980's. Nowadays it's the fad for certain rock stars to meet tribal chiefs in some part of the world where multi-nationals want to rape their land for oil and talk in those soft hippy tones of its meaning to the indigenous people in this really interesting place; only to do adverts for those multi-nationals so they can drive their big fuel guzzling cars all over the really interesting place whilst handing out freebie merchandising for their next business venture.

Yes. It's set against a backdrop of those early seventies trips to the East where there was talk of wisdom but only to return with goods they had purchased for virtually sod all or nicked and then to sell them at massively inflated prices on their market stall or in their growing legions of shops. This individualistic thinking has seemingly won through. The gimp (anorak) now owns the computer world. They are now kings in their own head and do not have to socialise with people who they cannot benefit from. All making a contribution to our culture that has helped to give the 'form over content' ethos presiding over us at present. The prog rock fashion back in those days of the early seventies meant sod all to me.

I saw many of the followers as junior army types in the way they called each other by their surnames and when referring to the groups in their flat monotone speech. "Oh, you know, I'm into 'Zappa', 'Tull', 'Man', 'Zeppelin', yeah ?" It remained an unknown thing to me, seeing it as grammar school rock. The groups were called bands. They didn't make singles and, if they did, the single became the best known thing they ever did as in the case of Hawkwind's Silver Machine. No, when talking to one of the student types in those days, they would mumble with derision against bands making singles as being too commercial.

Commercial ? I thought that strange when you considered that the brothers against bread heads toured in private jets, had their lady in tow wearing fourteen endangered species on her back as a coat, made inroads to buy entire islands and living in a house bigger enough to park the entire range of passenger jets of a medium sized airline company in the front room. They made albums which supposedly had a running concept, sometimes about goblins living in the pocket of King Arthur's dressing gown or whatever, which you had to buy in ten easy parts to have the collection because 'we're not commercial man'.

Not very much, the sneaky sods. Hippies and Margaret Thatcher, what's the difference ?

A seemingly delirium of tedious patches of labour and escaping with alcohol every evening continued. It was coming into the hot summer of 1976. I started a job as a petrol pump attendant in an Esso garage on the Uxbridge Road and Pete had heard of a group called The Ramones. It seemed uncanny. There was stuff out there and we were not alone. They struck a big chord in the way I felt. They might never have seen it or meant it the way I was interpreting it. They could have been a trendy bunch, I don't know but the inability to pronounce words appealed to me and a feeling of nothing is everything. We felt on the outside and having feelings of not being invited but it was okay because we now had a reason of our own. Not just a passing fashion or something fitting into a nights' entertainment. No, it was an identity. The music papers called it 'nihilistic' and 'minimalism'. I wasn't sure what that meant but it gave me a good feeling, outsiders and mental illness, dealing with anger in humour that maybe didn't translate that well in the mainstream world but having significance to my delirious mind.

Deux

Pete gave me the name 'Manic'. It was something to do with my personality and he then added 'Skull' as my head was shaven. The skinheads were not back in fashion at that time but there was a memory of them. I liked having my hair cropped. I was a young skinhead a few years before which of course seemed like a lifetime. The only other people having a shaved head or a 'number one' to be precise were people coming out of hospital after some kind of treatment or an operation which was a quip thrown at me by the older Sunday morning footballer types, sporting their clipped beards and a collection of hair styles straight out of a hair stylist's portfolio who had been sacked from having his work exhibited at Crufts. I had never liked the fashion for flared trousers but, unlike nowadays, there was not the choice. It was only flares. A lot of those Sunday morning, footballer types took a long time to shake themselves from their high-waisted flares and platypus looking platform soled shoes. Yes, those foolish flares. Forget all this bollocks about the stupid bloody things being cool. The sight of a forty five year old deputy bank manager in a bri-nylon shirt, a two bob tie, wispy greasy hair laying dank on the shoulders of a John Collier 'window to watch' (and that is all you were meant to do, just watch, don't buy) suit with flared trousers didn't look very cool and, if that was the manifestation of sixties counter culture revolution, someone had thrown a sick joke into the equation. And it was a common sight. However, to buy a pair of straight trousers was impossible. I suppose you could of got some if you went to a tailors to get a pair made or a theatrical place up the West End might provide a garment that only a few years previous was the standard wear on a gentleman's leg in any high street in the fucking western world.

I went to Foster Brothers in Uxbridge high street. They used to supply the uniforms for a couple of the local schools. It was a very old fashioned place having a damp rancid atmosphere of dust, staidness and homosexuality. After explaining my plight and hoping that they might have some old stock hanging around, the man found me a pair of grey, straight legged flannels. It did not occur to me to search out a shop that might be selling the old skinhead fashion

29

but I think they must have gone out of circulation a few years earlier. It seems strange, given that we live in the free world, that a pair of light grey flannel trousers could evoke such feelings of mockery, grudge and sometimes hate. Going into the bigot lounges, known as pubs, in the suburbs of one of the largest metropolitan areas on Earth, one would assume that there would exist a culture of accommodating different tastes and being a little acceptable to slight changes that might spring up in fashion. Yet, something as innocuous as those bloody trousers got me into scrapes that could easily have become violent. At the time I thought it funny, having a man dressed in a cheese clothe shirt, a bouffant hairstyle with a stench of a sticky spray to keep it in place, telling me that my trousers looked stupid. In less than a year, when playing down the Roxy, I was being asked where I got my trousers from as they looked great !

Pete and I started rehearsing. We were becoming more organised. Plug (Pete Edwards), who later became our roadie, sang for a rehearsal or two before Howard stepped in. Nigel, who came from a different musical taste, played the bass. Howard, Nigel, Pete Edwards and me all went to the same school; we were Abbotsfield boys, Pete Stride being the only one not going to the place. Howard, my brother Dave and Pete Edwards (Plug) had seen the Sex Pistols. Something was happening and it seemed good. What stayed with me about seeing the Pistols on that Bill Grundy news programme was the news item just before the show started. There had been trouble in Soweto, South Africa and many people had been killed. There was a film of these dead bodies, lying in a line. They looked very young and there was this army or police bloke kicking the heads of these dead young men. He was wearing shorts and what looked to me like wellington boots. I saw him kicking and stamping on the head of one of these boys/men. The news ended with a matter of fact roundup about one of the Royalty opening a college for flower pressing or whatever and then there was the weather forecast before going into the piece on the Sex Pistols show and of them swearing. The switchboards were crammed as never before with complaints because the sight and sound of these young men in a pop group had upset people's sensitivities. The members of the group were threatened personally with violence and, of course, it sold newspapers and records.

'Mm', I thought, 'be careful of the humans out there Pete. Their reasoning is very odd'. As far as I know the report from South Africa did not evoke complaints.

Yes, the worth of a man, indeed.

We started to rehearse but it was not the conventional beginnings that a young group starting out goes through. For one thing, we didn't do covers except for 'Then I kissed Her' which got changed almost immediately to 'Then I kicked Her' but believe me, there was no political or social agenda or trying to say something sexist or some such bollocks.

We got the gear around in the van that Nigel used at work. He always insisted that he was a television engineer. I doubted it then as I do now. We did a few rehearsals, doing our sound. Not one of us had experience of playing in groups and, looking back, our perception of what would be acceptable was a little off centre. "We're better than we sound," was my answer one night to a couple of people in another group who had come to rehearse at the same hall as us. "It's not what you think it sounds like," I think was Pete's response. This became a familiar line of defence throughout the coming few years.

We did not have a name but I always knew what the group should be called. There was a man, Paul, called 'Paul the coal man' who used to be a regular in our local pub The Coach and Horses. He was a massive bloke and I always thought of him as a great character. He often told me to, "shake the hand that shook the hand of the great Reg Dwight". He would then spit on his great mitt and hold it out for me to shake. It appealed to me, Paul, a bear of a man, always in his coal delivering clothes, proudly telling the tale of shaking Elton John's hand in a pub not far from where we came from. He used to call over to Pete and me, "The Lurkers, always in the corner, come on out of there and stand at the bar," waving a great arm at us and laughing. This large man's skin and clothing was dusted permanently from the dirt of his coal sacks. He was an imposing man who was a known drinker in various places. It seemed to me he was alone, gregarious, a hard man, physically if needed, far beyond the limits of the average nasty bastard hard man but he enjoyed the smiling side of a person's face. I would think as dark as his clothes and a big man who can spot and share the feelings of the small man. Pete wanted to call the group The Chains. I told him if we were called that I wouldn't be part of it. The Lurkers it was.

Our first gig was at Uxbridge Technical College, sometime in late 1976. It was the first time for all of us and we had no knowledge of the music etiquette, not knowing the rules so to speak. 'Lambs' might have been a better name. We supported Screaming Lord Sutch and we were lucky to have such a nice person to play with on our first outing. He must have thought 'We've got a right lot here' but he was supportive in letting us use their gear and moving stuff around the stage for us. Things that I was to learn was a point of power for most of the silly fuckers that inhabit rock 'n' roll with its pecking order and people vying for a position within its structure. Certain roadies I met along the way have exhibited all that is bad in the nature of us humans. It was a home gig for us but not that it mattered. The set lasted twelve minutes.

Dave, Lord Sutch, said to me, "Is that it ?"
"Yeah," I said.
"I thought it was one song," he said.

He asked us to play some more. I told him we didn't know any more and besides that, I was knackered. But, given a short rest we blasted through the same numbers again and if I remember rightly it was in a shorter amount of time. 'Practice makes perfect' I thought. Some local people had come to see us. They didn't like it, of course. Most were interested in the conventional rock scene, a kind of denim jacketed weekend rebel type of thing. It was the suburbs, they most probably wanted 'Free Bird' or 'Clapton' and the usual merge of white people whining through tunes they'd nicked from black people, having intellectualised it and conveniently leaving the black person out of the formula (only to be allowed in as an act of tokenism when time and place permitted). It all left me as cold and with as much feeling as morgue marble. And these people were very unforgiving to the 'punk scene' as they perceived it to derail, devalue and debunk their music and demoralise and destroy their ego. Good.

There were some well publicised scorn coming from the old wave. Rick Wakeman is a known example and I imagined him having friends who are most probably newscasters and journalists from local BBC television, doing programmes called 'Look Aylesbury, to manor house land' with the king or 'Wizard' with his culture that is the cutting edge of conventionality. The sort of thing which is carried on today by those rascal rebels who cook food on television and are more than welcome at dinner parties where discussions take place about bull fighting, hanging, shooting animals, money and power.

Anyway, excuse me there.

We encountered those jumping on the punk scene as it grew roots in changing fashion. They chopped their music to a minimalist sound, many adopting fake cockney voices but letting slip the words, 'right', 'cool' and 'sure' in their native student monotone. No, I suppose we were oddballs from suburbia. My rebellion was not the social one but one of dealing with mental illness, played out to what I imagined was a receptive social setting, having a struggle to identify. Punk gave me a platform except it was not how it is formally understood.

We started to rehearse in a basement of a record shop down the North End

Road in Fulham. The shop was one of a few shops called Beggar's Banquet - Martin Mills and Nick Austin owned them. I think they got the idea from Richard Branson. It was a kind of student appeal of selling and buying second hand records, the records graded as to their quality. The manager of the shop in Fulham was Mike Stone. Mike was twenty eight years old at the time. Of course, I thought him an old bloke, he was an old mod and his favourite group was The Who. For some reason he saw a Pete Townsend quality in Pete Stride's music. If I remember rightly, Mike was soon to get himself married and, as they say, settle down. The Lurkers inspired in Mike an impetus to get involved with a group, something he had always wanted to do. I think he had done some DJ-ing. Having a life long interest in music and managing a shop seemed to be the ceiling to his involvement. He came from the North, Leeds and had plans of going back up north but, unlike most people of his age who were involved in music, he saw the punk development as exciting. What with his memories of The Who and his energy as a sixteen year old youth in Leeds, he was a man denying the 'whack' in himself. To most people we sounded like a row but Mike saw a place in the music world for us. He asked his two bosses to come down and listen to us, explaining to them what was happening in the music scene. They didn't seem interested and didn't really know what was happening. In their thinking, Ry Cooder, Joe Walsh and having a clap and sing along with Bread was an adequate cultural offering required for an intelligent youth rebellion. But Mike persisted. He bought an old Bedford van and offered his time to drive the gear and us around. Nigel had left his job so the van also went.

Mike would have started up his own label if he had the money but as it was he had faith. I should think that if we hadn't met Mike, we might not have got a recording contract because we were not the aspiring art school bunch and we were not the opportunistic proficient musicians seeing an angle to grind their axe, man. We played a couple of places like The Roxy which was a salient venue in the emerging punk scene. It was whilst we were playing there that Arturo saw us play. Mike told us that he knew a bloke who liked the group. Things were not working with Nigel, I am sorry to say. It was a couple of things. He didn't seem to hit it with the music, different influences, put it like that. Nigel left and formed his own group. He always had his ideas of how things should sound and wrote his own stuff. Anyway, we're all inadequate lunatics, it was dealt with like adults of course and then Arturo joined.

I would go straight to rehearsals from working in the garage wearing my Esso shirt, so Art called me 'Esso'. At a few places we played, people used to shout out 'Esso Blue'. It was a long time ago and the memory of the Esso advert was still in people's minds. It stuck, Manic Esso it was.

Mike asked Martin and Nick to manage us and try to get us a record contract. They eventually agreed to manage us but getting us signed was not as easy as Mike thought. We might have been one of the first punk groups but there was a spilling of proper groups into the scene. The Lurkers were anomalous and did not translate, unlike groups that simply changed their hairstyle and the chords to their songs. They were presentable. When the thing clicked to mainstream, these people had the ability to offer a breadth and willingness to change style in order to adapt. And it wasn't just our music that was quirky. Mike could not believe that nearly all of us went to the same school and lived with our mums in suburbia. I thought having Art in the group might give us credence in the eyes of the music types. He had been down in Wales after being depressed and bored in his native Fulham area; got even more bored whilst slipping into the dullness of an outlying hippy idea and returned to London on hearing the change in the music. But, he came back to London and lived with his mum. Crazy guys those punk rock demons.

When going to some of the gigs, we felt the outsider amongst the outsiders in rock music. Sometimes, Generation X used to rehearse down our basement in Fulham. They were conscious of their behaviour, mindful to their duty to fashion. Many of the groups had histories in music. This was for many just another beat, a change of jacket and trousers, that's all. I had the one beat, the drummer of Generation X pointed this out to me as he popped along with his rocky, funky sounding offbeat, double up, flange out; bit like being in the company of some boring fucker who is a fan of Phil Collins and when I think of it, I most probably was.

"The Lurkers ?", "Who are they ?", "Where are they from ?" Those became familiar comments but I was undeterred. I remember the drummer of Slaughter and The Dogs in our early days down The Roxy taking the piss about my snare drum playing. He said, "Do you like John Bonham ?" "Yeah," I said, making out I knew something when I didn't know the sound and didn't fucking care, silly fuckers.

Looking back, I remember Pete never having any spare strings. For groups playing in places in town, there would be planning and a sense of performance. I remember Paul Weller, when playing down the Red Cow with The Jam, giving Pete some strings and Paul's Dad asking if we needed a spanner or something for the drums. They must have thought 'here come the cowboys from way out west'. They were organised. We just stumbled into the scene, grinning, saying all the wrong things and not having a clue. Looking back, they were good to us. I remember Paul Weller's dad asking me if we changed into stage clothing. This confused me. We moved from the bar to the stage and back to the bar again. The Jam had their suits in sealed bags. They were an act and very good at it they were as well. We might have appeared arrogant in our shrugging off such matters as unimportant but the fact was we didn't understand that one needed strings and all that stuff. So getting a record deal was hard. A & R guys had groups like 'Renaissance' playing on their personal deck. They clipped their flares and beards in the afternoon and they did not pow-wow with outsiders. When meeting us, there were no terms of reference and our music did not speak in broad contemporary statements but rather in a claustrophobic naivety with songs having a natural acceptance that girls were objects and connected to anxiety and shooting people.

> Martin Mills and Nick Austin formed Beggars Banquet Records Ltd
> and signed us up. A charitable act.

We went into a small recording studio. I think it was near Heathrow airport and we recorded 'Shadow' and 'Love Story' in a couple of hours and I think we were playing that evening. What I do remember was the English branch of The Eagles fan club that owned and worked in the studio. There was no humour or enthusiasm on their part, just a near disgust and regarding us as an irritant that was not to be taken seriously. Yet, in a matter of months, the beardy boring brigade was to suffer a gross intrusion into their cosy world of bean bag rock as the punk sound gave music a good kick up the arse.

We started playing the pubs and various places in London like The Vortex, The Kensington, The Nashville and The Roundhouse that were accommodating the punk scene. One evening, during the week, we played with The Police down the Marquee. There were people down to see us but there wasn't for The Police, save for a few professional looking people. They had a different guitarist then and they had not adopted the reggae influence. They sounded like a traditional group of musicians doing a switch of fashion to change direction in their career, gelling up their hair, etc. I knew sod all about most things and showed my great perceptive powers and judgement when speaking to their drummer Stuart Copeland in the bar. He was and is I suppose, tall and American. Before The Police, he played in a group called Curved Air with whom he had minor success. I later found out his family were connected and occupied positions in this great society of ours, so I expounded my massive insight when he asked me what I thought of his group. I told him, "Well mate, I'm not being nasty or anything but you won't get anywhere with a name like The Police." "Oh, why's that ?" he asked, leaning back in a confident manner. I rambled on about something. He watched me in a judgmental way as if he thought it interesting, maybe to tell one of his well heeled friends, say a psychoanalyst, at one of his dinner parties. They had a purpose about them. They drank cartons of orange and seemed like the bright boys at school. They were.

Unlike The Lurkers, the other groups were not coming out of the starting blocks so to speak, The Damned, The Jam, The Pistols, etc. Their music had a traditional rock structure and, as I said, experience and influence from playing standards to learn their craft. I used to tell people Mo Tucker was a good drummer when we were accused of not being very good, saying I'm not interested in being judged in the boring debate of who is and isn't a 'good player man' or I said some such bull as a feeble defence for not being able to play a conventional rock drum pattern. But, all the same, we were not very good. We were just learning. Anyway, that's my excuse; 'it's better than you think it sounds'.

However, when it came to drinking beer and being consistent about the business of having a drink, we had an edge on many. I might not have been in groups playing standards in pubs but I had been in pubs everyday of my life from fifteen years of age honing another artistic craft. But when it came to drinking shipments, Howard Wall was surely a true master of the discipline. Always approaching the session in an understated manner, quietly spoken, a keen eye to detail and always considered that money spent on food was money wasted. One evening down The Nashville, a pub next door to West Kensington station that we played regularly, Howard started about six o'clock, that being the evening opening time in those days, downing nineteen pints of Extra Special Brew, ESB which, at that time, was considered a strong drink and complaining that the last bell was being a burden, as if stopping him popping out for a chat and a pint.

I don't think we drank a lot because of being nervous of playing, not on my part anyway, it was more to do with an idea of missing out on going out for the night and having a drink. Playing the drums in a pub wasn't going to get in my way and, looking back, I see that the drink thing did hold Howard, Pete and myself back, in place, to one side, or whatever. I didn't think about it but four pints would have to be next to my kit for me to feel ready to play and gigs were often held up whilst drinks were brought from the bar and having to be paid for with the soggy note from my sweat soaked jeans. At times it was frustrating trying to get a drink from my position behind the drums, an aspect of playing in a group which I would tell people who had come to see us. The music was often towards the back of priorities. Mistakes or cock ups were grinned away, as having a good night was seen as having greater importance than such boring, poncy, postmortem trials of who played a bum note and was it in time. Fuck me, I would have joined a real group if I wanted to be bored to death.

Talking of ESB reminds me of the front cover of our first single, Shadow. It was a photograph of us standing outside the Red Cow pub on a night that we were playing down there. I was standing there holding my drink as the photo was taken and a group of children about eight years of age came walking by making remarks and being cheeky. Then one little girl asked if she could have a swig of my drink. I handed her my mug which was over half full of ESB. She downed the lot then gave me the empty glass and walked off sniggering with her mates. On the cover, I'm looking at the empty glass, contemplating my lost drink as the photo is taken. Another one of my successful dates. She's most probably still alive, had a few kids, seven marriages and I am still lamenting about that lost drink.

Arturo (Art) and myself did not present a physical image fitting the decadent, posturing, fashionable, starving, lean, precious artist at the cutting edge of trendy fashion having his gaunt, delicate self and ego coaxed by his agent and loved one from his attic to a waiting public. I suppose to the arty crowd we were seen as having an image of buffoon rock, not the crazy rock and rollers. One gig we played in the north of the country, Accrington working man's club I think, Art spotted that they were selling pies for twelve pence each. It was too good a bargain to miss. We had six each before going on to play. Comfort food has played a big part in it all for me and has been a shared theme in my relationship with Art over the years.

On getting to know Art, we found that we had some things in common. Although I am sure Art told me that he was a Fulham fan when we first met, it transpired that he is in fact a Chelsea fan. He comes from the Fulham area. His dad came from the same area in Fulham as my dad. Also, Art had bunked off school to see Chelsea in the FA Cup replay against Leeds at Manchester in 1970. I went with two mates from school although being a Fulham supporter and bought a fifteen shilling standing ticket on the train for thirty shillings; that's seventy five pence and £1.50p in new money. It didn't leave me with much money and we tried to sleep on the floor at Euston when the train got back to London and from there I had to bunk the train fare back home when the underground trains started in the morning except I didn't go straight home but to the newsagents where I did a paper round. I told the man who ran the shop that I had been to the game the night before but he wasn't interested. On leaving the shop, I found an old shopping trolley and put my papers in that. It made the job easier as the bag was heavy. Now, there was a school in the road that I did my paper round and all the young yobs came by me shouting insults at the odd boy pushing the shopping trolley. I told them that I had been to the game the previous night but they started chanting derisive remarks as they didn't believe me. Part of the dress worn at that time for the young skinhead included a Harrington jacket. They were usually black, some dark blue, dark green or a Prince of Wales check. Art told me that he had a canary yellow Harrington which obviously stood out. I thought this might be significant as my Harrrington was pink. A pink jacket was not what one would imagine residing comfortably with the skin culture. Yet, years later the skin fashion was to be embraced by certain gay men to project that masculine geezer image. Anyhow, years later Art told me that he had the video of the game and swears he can see himself holding up a scarf in the Stretford End.

I was close to Art when playing in the group although all along I knew we were not what he wanted. He and I would have stupid arguments. One that has stayed with me is another memory exemplifying our interests and concerns on matters of lofty decadence. One morning, we all met at the shop in Fulham for the drive up to Barrow-in-Furness. Art had gone into the bakery and bought himself a pie. I asked if I could have a bite and from then on, for most of the journey in the back of the Bedford van, a subject of severe gravity was bitterly debated. Art would not give me a bite of his pie. "You have the money, I have the money, I had the inclination," he said this maybe thirty times in that six odd hour drive. To question the use of the word inclination was never brought up during those hours of conflict.

During those early gigs we started to get a following, namely the 'Fulham Crew' with characters such as Max and Eddie and there was also the 'Kingston Crew', a crowd in part seeking their own reputation but loyal to us which, when one considers some of the places we played, was very supportive. The two first singles, 'Shadow' and 'Freak Show' sold well. As with other groups at that time if the same amount was sold today they would be top ten hits. We did a few John Peel sessions, he seemed to be a Lurker fan or said he was. The first session was in 1977. We recorded four in all and were pleased about them in all ways, from the engineering to John Peel playing them for us. It did seem a bit like a stuffy school, I mean the BBC with its system and structure. The recording technology was a throwback with the young man working as a junior assistant to the junior of the main assistant who, in turn, was the junior to Engineer's Assistant, then the Engineer with all eyes towards the Producer, usually an outsider brought in to do the session. That being said, they got a good sound and were good to us. On an early session, whilst putting the delicate final touches to the ending of a song, Be My Prisoner (I believe), Mike Stone rattled his car keys in front of the microphone telling the producer, "A trick I learned from Phil Spector." The producer looked across the line of juniors and assistants. He watched their expressionless faces giving no response. He then looked back to Mike and nodded slowly.

Those sessions were our main publicity. Young men across this land and women I hope but it was not my experience to meet many (hardly any) women who were Lurker fans, would lay in bed listening to the John Peel show with the excitement of knowing that they had access to a music that was different from the current contemporary scene. They had an identity with groups often having obscure sounding names, taping them and adding them to a personal library making up their music. It was great to meet some of these people at places we played, people having a deep knowledge of indie music, asking me questions concerning the group on matters of such specific detail that I would more often than not stare at them, shake my head dumbly and ask if they wanted a drink, which most did not, being thoughtfully focused, drinking a half of shandy or "just a coke, please". A world of quiet people, ordered, with plans, schedules and dates, aside from the throng, watching on, noticing with a singular observation, not participating with the crowd but inwardly empires were being built and destroyed. A record cover in a plastic bag in one hand, the other holding a small glass of coke, a light reflects on one lens of his glasses, I look again and he's gone.

We were one of the groups from the early punk movement that worked with an evangelical zeal, going to places that were untarnished territories, often suffering personal humiliation, ridicule and sometimes finding an attitude one would expect adopted for a party of visiting aliens. It was summer 1977 and our 'on the ball' management, Beggar's Banquet, showed insight, imagination and knowledge. A budding punk group on their hands beckoned the question, 'Where should we send them ? Berlin ? Paris ? Milan ? New York ? Well, Manchester ? Sheffield ?' Nah, we'll send them to the Isle of Arran. Three nights on the Isle of Arran.

On arriving there we met a supporter of ours, a bloke called Walt Davidson. Walt was a keen photographer in his spare time but his main job was for the post office. Walt travelled alone far and wide, not only to see us but also taking his photographs of other groups. He was a good chap. His first line when meeting us was of his find in the back of a scout hut which was to be our first gig. He had found, ironically enough, a pogo stick. Walt couldn't believe that we were playing there. It was a Glasgow holiday, fortnight kind of affair called Paisley fortnight, I think. The crowd was long-haired, flare-trousered wearing Scots on rocket fuel having an uneasy relationship with enjoying themselves and smashing a glass in someone's face. However, they were alright although not that receptive and didn't want to hear something they did not know, like a lot of people I suppose. Still, we weren't beaten up and that could be seen as our perk for doing the jaunt. But, those boys at Beggar's Banquet certainly had their finger on the pulse.

In the summer of 1977, we played Paisley in Glasgow. Glasgow was a good place for us. The gig in Paisley was called The Silver Thread Hotel. A chap called Kenny Crawford jumped on the stage and started head butting the bass guitar. He stood there in his kilt, blood coming from a gash on his head telling me how great he thought it was. It came to being that Kenny was a bit of a known character from Maryhill in Glasgow and someone I would meet again although, at this time, I didn't know his name.

The places and areas having a name for being rough were usually kind to us, being more receptive than the conventional marginal music places. I was learning that these marginal places were structured with codes of coolness and people having a bibliographic cultural history which had to be passed for acceptance, a crowd which were arty, being part of the intellectual movement of the day. No, they didn't accept us. We found it odd at first, considering our songs were not about football crowd violence. We did not incite hoards of young men to fight and see themselves as aligned to gangs. We had no preconceived plan of being a 'beer and lads' group. Our songs were of the little person at odds with themselves and the world in which they found themselves. We did not have the sales pitch or a natural tendency to fawn or want to be with boring facile wankers. We did not jump on the next arriving gravy train whether it be eco-friendly to do with one's sexual preference or using a three minute pop song to challenge foreign policy and peoples' responses to each other, whatever their race or colour. I learned that, for a lot of people in groups, it was a career, just like those sneaky fuckers I had met at work, reeking of mediocrity once you lifted their cover of deceit, having schemes and designs that were to be strictly adhered to. The hippy types were reclaiming the inner cities, fresh from their exploitative experiences in places like Wales. Swapping their pot-making skills and habits of inserting a musical pipe up their nose, blowing it and believing that other people should be interested and listening to music that never raised itself above its smug, self self-possessed comfort.

Excuse me for what could be considered a rant now but here goes. It is my experience to find most of these muso, trendy, hippy types to be very rude and I mean in the old fashioned sense, yet they are able to turn on the charm in order to get something. I remember, before the punk thing came along, going to see groups and being elbowed at the bar by some lanky tosser in crushed velvet or an afghan and stinking of some incense stuff. Entertaining a Puerto Rican or a South Mulacan or whatever or whoever would be culturally fashionable, a token for dinner party discussions, transited from the setting of the communal fire or squat to their parents' house. One week these tossers are in their squat, passing the liberated, neurotic free bean sprout and the cake made from the dick of a dead Tibetan sherpa; the next week it's round to their relatives for a wedding meal and tuck into partridge pie and blood bags or something. Yes, the shift from squat discussions to articulations around their oak table later in life, just like their father's, it all looked to me like a natural course in the maintenance of conservatism.

In that first year of being around, we played with The Stranglers and very pleasant they were as well. Although their company charged groups to support them, it wasn't only The Stranglers but other groups who had a name and they would charge people to go on tour with them. I remember they didn't charge us for the gig we did with them but when I raised this as I considered it a bit of a liberty, I was told by the hippy/punksters that it gave public attention, etc., etc., et-fucking etc. I thought, 'they know it all, these middle class teacher, social worker types, they ask you your opinion, you give an answer and they then tell you why you are wrong'. I'm sure that if we had a bit of a name for ourselves, we wouldn't have charged anyone to play with us or support us. We didn't when reaching the humble status of having a support group, not that it had anything to do with an allegiance to a political dogma, we just thought that sort of thing was bad manners.

Mind, that's why some of these fuckers now drive around in cars worth the same amount of money as a Third World Country's debt and I'm still going on about fairness. Anyway, in the main, the group was playing the right places, at the cutting edge, as they say.

For a while we supported The Jam down The Red Cow on Wednesday nights, then with 999, we played with Generation X a few times, once I remember at The Roundhouse. All good stuff but I mean, something was wrong. It felt that we were distanced from what was going on and a certain kind of person would seem to figure more and more in my life; the loner, 'our fan', and this felt good. They aligned themselves with us as if it was war.

Playing one's own material is completely different from playing covers. The person in the pub usually wants what he or she knows and, for the majority, having their mind up for them seems the norm. It's safe. They can associate with what they know and an unknown presence is a threat and this is what we did to a lot of people who witnessed our row on their evening out. And this provincial culture has won through at this present time as cover bands and television programmes use elaborate karaoke to make instant stars and there's a heavy influence of the parents in the kitchen deciding what their children will be dancing to at their party in the living room. At times, it felt like I was going out of my way to make life difficult for myself. I certainly had no ideas of shocking people or getting under their skin in that arty way of wearing ragged clothing and performing in a manner that was meant to present insubordination. But the punk thing was a new style and it did intimidate. I also believe it has had a massive influence right up to present day culture, not only in music but also in dress, style and attitude, all being part of a political and social change occurring in 1970's Britain.

Back then, the reception was often less than warm when turning up in the provincial pub and playing our own stuff. There would be the person who does the lights who knows someone who met someone once who met this person who used take a dog for a walk that belonged to a person who has now died but was the brother-in-law of a bloke who auditioned for a group in the sixties that Eric Clapton rehearsed with once ! So, having that setting the scene for artistic value and acceptance, the sight of the 'differents' coming through the door and not being able to play always evoked contempt from the provincial puppets. They would sometimes threaten violence or be just rude.

Besides Arturo, none of us in the group had travelled much and not around the towns of this country. I saw Fulham play away as a youngster but really that was about it. One of the interesting things for me was to go to the Northern towns that I had heard on the tele, on Saturdays, as a child watching the wrestling hosted by Kent Walton. His thick creamy, strangely sounding North American accent introducing us to the 'Bradford Baths' and the 'Halifax Town Hall'. "Welcome grappling fans," he would say. Later in life I would listen to the voice of Eddie Waring presenting rugby league on Saturday lunchtimes. I would be watching whilst having a terrible hangover, listening to that voice of his, an echo from the Northern country's heavy industrial past, "He's a big strapping lad from Pontefract, played for Castleford and lost his teeth at St Helens." It seemed a delirium, listening to his accent, what with the effect of the drink from the night before, an ashtray spilling over, a film of sweat, greased mouth, feeling queasy and disorientated. There was a world out there with those places having those people doing those things, all distant, at times giving a feeling of comfort but always waiting for the day to pass so I could go to a pub and forget.

The obvious insults and prejudices were thrown at us for being Southerners or cockneys and, add to it, the punk factor with all the negativity that that aroused, it was often a back footed advance into these territories. That Bedford van of Mike Stone's would slowly wheel itself up and down the concrete arteries of this country. I would think sometimes about what place would dislike us least. We had some good nights but, generally, I believe it would be true to say that it was grim. As I have said, we were primarily out of sorts with the customary group culture and the group itself did not feel as one. Arturo was not at ease with The Lurker philosophy and our attitude. I was not that happy myself, Howard rarely spoke and the feel became bleak.

Albeit, we chugged to places like Ruffus's in Manchester. Remember it was mid-week and the United Kingdom was in a rundown to cataclysmic social change. The place was tired and dirty, the club was run by and for West Indians. I didn't know who booked these things but that thought went through my mind as I sat behind the drums looking out over a tiny dance area and across an empty floor to a deserted bar and there, that evening, standing with his arms folded a large West Indian frowns with a mixture of disbelief, disinterest and obviously not liking what he is hearing. That night in the club called Ruffus, there was a barman, a doorman and a white woman. None of them were about to work on the Samaritan switchboard later that evening. We got through the second or third number when the barman couldn't take any more, coming up to the stage waving his hands in front of his face, he shook his head in a defeated manner and told me that it was to be an early exit. Whilst packing away my drums, I saw him give Mike Stone a cheque for fifty pounds. I knew it would bounce as high as we would if we offered a word of objection. The cheque was made of rubber. It didn't matter but what became a constant in my mind during that time was, 'who booked us there ?' And the other places that we played that were so absurdly, well, wrong ?'

In essence, we were white boys from the suburbs venturing into cultures where the only knowledge we had of them was the shallow and slanted one presented on the television or whatever.

A place called the 777 club in Lancaster was another exemplary 'miss booking'. The manager was a big fat bloke. Like a lot of Northerners I met, his idea of humour was to be plain insulting. A crowd of mainstream culture types ambled up for their weekend entertainment, dressed in their new shirts and medallions.

The women looking like they were going to a wedding or court as they all crawled around the manager, the big boss man, because there was fuck all else around for entertainment except for his khazi of an establishment which was about the size of an average corner shop. He said, "All the way from London, these cunts, spunk rockers they call themselves, why bother." Placing the letter 's' in front of the word punk kept this charming man with an intelligent wit amused all evening as he entertained to the desperate gallery of big grin small thought vessels called people.

That joke was common around the Northern towns, that clever play on word. Although sometimes there were those who didn't use it in mockery, a sweaty face at the end of an oven hot gig would occasionally push into me saying, "If that's spunk rock, I'll have it."

When I asked the management how was it we played so many of these 'miss booking's, I was told it is a 'risky business' and 'you have to do your apprenticeship'. But this wasn't cruise ship cover specials on tour, waiting to get a break backing Jim Davidson on a tour of army bases. We were supposed to be a young group involved in a vibrant new intrusion into the music world at the dawning of a cultural storm. I didn't find out who the people were doing this elaborate work on 'miss booking's in order for us to serve an apprenticeship; a word and term itself which was rapidly losing any meaning in a country that was on the edge of a major transformation in industrial relations, working practises and expectations.

The group itself was also going through a change, meaning it had run its course for Arturo being in The Lurkers. Art came from a more mainstream musical background, not a pop fan, more bluesy, prog-rock and folky. The punk scene brought him back to London where he became fan number one of The Stranglers. We were the mummy boys from suburbia. Art had flown from the nest a little and embraced cultural interests we did not adhere to. Art played in The Lurkers for seven months. We did two singles together, Shadow and Freakshow before he headed off with his own group, Pinpoint. Art had his own writing. It was not accommodated in The Lurkers. He grew outside of us and, at times, critical of our suburban neurosis and claustrophobic make up. But, that's us I suppose. That's why and what we were, The Lurkers. I'm still close to Art. We have similarities in our backgrounds and I feel shared feelings to the way of things. Always conscious of one's own insecurity and the mental moods that ensue from it, Art has a catalogue of songs that reveal this but they were to be played out in another structure.

We got a new bass player. Kim Bradshaw who had played in The Saints joined us. I liked The Saints. Some might say their feel wasn't a million miles from our sound. They were 'out of towners', really out of town, from Brisbane Australia. How we met Kim, I forget. It could have been through an article in Record Mirror where his girlfriend or partner, Rosalind Russell worked. She was an editor, I think. Anyway, Kim came down for an audition. It didn't take long and he was in. We had the two singles out and they had done well, not in the way The Rolling Stones or Elton John would consider well but, in a culty, independent way, it was good. I think Shadow sold twenty thousand in the first two weeks of its release and we were what they called a 'hard working group'. The gigs were generally rough and the 'miss booking's at times made it bizarre but The Lurkers were forging ahead in their own way.

As I've said, we were not that well accepted by the trendy bunch and, when we played with some of the people around, our difference became obvious. We played with Adam and the Ants down a club called Eric's in Liverpool. They had Jordan there with them, a person from the Chelsea art brigade. I doubt if she was at Old Trafford for the cup final replay in 1970. She might have been but we didn't talk about it. Some of these people existed in their world where egomania abounds and they were surrounded by lackeys who enjoyed their position of servitude. We also played with the likes of Holly Johnson who, at that time, played in arty groups in the Northern clubs. When I spoke to them, I felt like I was the bloke concreting their path or something like that.

We did two or three of gigs with The Buzzcocks, running consecutive nights up north. We supported them, the gigs went well and I liked some of their songs but they were a miserable bunch of sods. I remember speaking to Peter Shelly, trying to be polite, thinking I got on with him. It was difficult because he was a posy sort of bloke. Anyway, at the end of these nights, there was a note slipped under our door. On it was a scrawled message, 'My dear Lurkers, thanks for your support and fuck off'. I couldn't be certain who wrote it as we had enough abuse. That wasn't the problem but, thinking it might be some simpering little bastard doing a sneaky act, roused me into wanting to know who did this. It might not have been a member of the group but I would have dearly liked to have found out who the sneaky fucker was. The Lurks make more friends.

At that time our record company had been approached by a young man called Gary Numan. He had a group called Tubeway Army. They were a fairly heavy guitar, riffy sounding bunch, provincial people, with Gary's dad being a main force and support behind the group. In a way, a bit like Paul Weller's dad who was always at those early gigs down The Roxy and The Red Cow when we played with them. Tubeway Army supported us around places as Beggar's Banquet were trying to put on a package of their musical offering and one of their packages didn't particularly fit with the punk scene. Beggar's Banquet liked this chap called 'Ivor Biggun'. He sang quirky little songs having double innuendo and had a following of friends who had perpetual smiles for him and his involvement in this punk thing. He was a professional type. It was 'jolly good fun' I'm sure but I thought it came across a bit odd. The package was a bit like variety night down the local Wheel Tappers Club or the like.

It was beginning to seem that if we didn't have a 'miss booking', we would create one ourselves, a novel twist having inherent contradictions on the path of gaining success in the cool, new world out there. I mean Ivor was nice bloke and good luck to him but him singing 'I'm a wanker' to a chorus of thirty year old computer engineers and their wives on a night out made me ask serious questions of our management's reasoning. Their perspicacity was also in question with their dealing of Gary Numan, offering him only a distribution deal as they didn't think he was a safe bet. Gary paid the recording costs for his early stuff and later went on to be a life changing element in the lives of those running Beggar's Banquet records. It was only through the insistence of Mike Stone to get themselves involved in a new wave of music that their present success is due. It got them managing a group and overseeing the recording of a group's material. The other world of music that they were used to was a safe distance from the embryonic stages and all the painful growing that it entails.

Yes, The Lurks gave Beggar's Banquet a foot on the ladder and
Gary Numan took them on top of the building.

As for The Lurkers, our world of reality was played out in small venues around the country and usually, experiencing aggressiveness and witnessing unpleasant images that I found upsetting.

We had evenings down Bones Club in Reading where, as in other places, the locals often targeted the Fulham Crew. On one night a fight broke out. Steve, one of the Fulham boys, was trying to calm the situation when a bouncer hit him squarely on the back of his head with a long piece of four by two wood. Steve teetered about but was fine. I often jumped into a fracas. Don't get me wrong, I have a deep yellow stripe running down my back called 'survival' but, sometimes, one has to get involved when an injustice over a liberty is taking place. It was the violence and aggression when playing around places that soured it all for me. I didn't realise that I lived in a country where in every town night time entertainment is heavy with fear and spite. It was fuelling or fanning an anxiety already in place, going deeper, so that it tainted most things for me. I grew to view my fellow species with greater suspicion as I witnessed their antics and behaviour of cowardly aggression that is often dealt with as a joke and quipped at but for me it carried a far greater weight. Why people develop certain fears, obsessions or whatever is an industry in itself, yet states of mind born through direct experience are quite easy to understand.

For reasons I do not know, I detached myself from conventional sixteen year old activities and so avoided many situations that brought me into areas of confrontation and competition. I did not go to parties where there were people of my age but would drink in pubs with people often older than myself. On one such evening in a particularly unforgiving area of Hayes, Middlesex, a couple of blokes I had been with were invited to a party. I sensed hostility and most things wrong with humanity. I might have been sixteen but I had experience of this type of thing. To cut it short, as we stood in the garden of this house, about a dozen blokes, most in their early twenties, came streaming out of the door and windows and set about beating us up. The garden of this desirable property, in prime location, had deep holes dug in it and was covered by scaffold boards. One of my friends just disappeared down a hole as kicks, punches and insults rained down upon him. I saw my other friend receiving similar treatment and then I felt the mud beneath my feet thump against my back as I looked up at five or six of them kicking me. I then experienced disorientation, as if sucked into a timeless vacuum where there was cursing and the sound of splintering cracks on my face with the bitter taste of bile and blood that accompany them, along with the sharp shooting of flashing lights sparked in bursts from the blows that I received on my head. It seemed to go on for ages but most probably didn't. I lifted myself up from the grass and slowly realised that it was quiet and that I was in a different garden. I peered over a hedge and found that I was in the next door garden. I couldn't see my two friends so I stumbled down the road. A black cab was passing. He slowed, looked at me and stopped. He asked me if I wanted to go to hospital. I told him I wanted to go home. I was nearly deaf and my view of the life around me was blurred and there was a weird warm deep buzzing underneath it all. Without exaggeration, it was six months before the joints in my jaw were not painful and didn't click as I opened my mouth. Not long afterwards I heard that one of these blokes who was kicking me in that garden was killed in Amsterdam. I was told that a bus had mounted the pavement and ran him over. Good, I'd like to buy that bus driver a drink.

This incident contributed to my fear and distrust of the 'straight-back', town centre, chain store, designer clothes-wearing, male, shit head. Becoming used to social avoidance, meaning steering clear of certain social practices, I found that playing in a group occupying a marginal appeal in the loving towns of this country was getting to me. It felt to be a seemingly unrelenting sphere of aggression and the acceptance of grim behaviour gnawed deeper and deeper, so much so that, at the beginning of the year when we played in a small place called Mr George's in Coventry, I thought I had had enough of it all and I also thought that I was plunging into some kind of breakdown.

The club was packed. It was nearly a 'miss booking'. Some people had come along to see us but it was essentially a straight-back, meeting place, a rutting centre, an experimental farm, another of the Broadmoor outreach clinics dotted around that pass themselves off as places of leisure where people spend their quality time doing churlish barbarism. During the afternoon, I wandered about the City centre in that drained and dreary way, always tired and having a propensity for nose bleeds that last longer than a matinee performance down one's local cinema. I looked around the buildings and the people, thinking of the damage inflicted upon it and them during the Second World War. I felt a lost kind of melancholy. Not knowing history, I looked into the faces of the older people who might have been around, seeing if there were any clues to those awful experiences. But, night must fall as they say and out came the new generation. Welfare State nurtured, with the parental guiding wisdom of post war social engineering with its intentions of betterment for all and fully laden on school milk, inside toilets, the excesses of food and labour which allows some money in one's pocket or purse to express a civic right for going out and socialising with one's neighbours. Those fun loving, glad to be free creatures that were in Mr George's that night, for me, formed and forged an amplified symbol which was an ugly fearful image of others.

Before we played there had been an incident. I heard a crash, some glass smash, a small cheer that quickly gave way to laughter and there, being dragged through the crowd by his feet was a fat young man with a Teddy boy haircut. His unconscious frame bumped on the ground exposing a soft stomach that wobbled. The sight caused people to laugh. One young woman standing with a group pointed at him, hardly able to contain herself, a glass in one hand, the finger of the other pointing at the disarrayed youth, laughing, drawing breath only to chant words of scorn. I looked around myself and thought 'who really cares and would it have mattered if Mr Hitler's bombs extinguished this semblance of life from our sad old blue planet ?'

A few days later we played a college, polytechnic or whatever it was in Leicester. It wasn't really home territory and a lot of the people there were objective glass throwers, gobbers and abusers, behaviour learned from the various arms of the great body media. We were approached by someone who asked if it would be alright for his friend to sit at the side of the stage when we played later that night. His friend was a man who I would guess was in his mid to late twenties, blind and bound to a wheelchair. He was a big music fan, having heard our radio session for John Peel he had record sleeves that he wanted signing. We decided, because of the raucous behaviour of the crowd, that it would be best if he sat behind the group as we played, it being a large stage with a curtain cutting the depth in half. As we played, bottles, cans and glasses were thrown at us. Maybe our greatest luck was that none of us during those rowdy gigs got killed or at least lost sight of an eye or whatever but some nights I did get hit by a flying missile. The spitting, because there was so much of it, used to find its target though. Sometimes I would get caught in the mouth, eye and it was annoying if the phlegm of someone with chronic bronchial problems or issues spat and it caught my hand, the slimy fluid would make holding the drum stick difficult. After some gigs, I could peel a veritable sheet of phlegm and dark multi coloured mucus from the front of my T-shirt. It would be layered, a greasy accumulation of nasal and chest congestion, a gift from the aspiring accountants, bricklayers and soon to be dead people of this great land. Many of the singers playing to the punk audiences would get so fed up with the spitting that they would throw down the microphone and shout at the crowd. Howard had his own method. One night, not saying anything to the rest of us, he pulled a water pistol from his Mac pocket and fired at the main culprits. I wondered, what was in the water pistol?

So, on that night in Leicester, a man sat in his wheel chair on the stage behind a curtain, an unseen non-seeing witness to the event. I took the odd peek at him through a slit in the curtain. There he was in the shadow, only hearing but also feeling.

A recording studio had been identified in a place called Kempsey in Worcester. We drove there straight from playing The Marquee, a good gig for us, arriving at this little pub in the middle of the night that was to be our accommodation during the recording of our LP. The studio was just across the road from the pub. Our producer was Mick Glossop who hadn't previously produced anyone before but had worked as an engineer on Frank Zappa stuff and other worthy musician types. Mick had been a head sound engineer for Richard Branson's concern, a big place in Oxford and The Townhouse studio down the Goldhawk Road in West London. Mick was a nice bloke. I'm sure he thought us a strange bunch but it seemed a challenge to this very professional boffin of the buttons. He was polite at all times and must of thought it odd that a group had such, speaking for myself first here, little experience and musicianship skills. We had a sound of our own and bashed into it at full tilt but, all the same, as I say, it must have been a challenge and one he rose to. He later worked with The Skids and The Ruts but most of these groups, as I have mentioned, had played a variety of music and some of them had played in quasi Stones types of groups, emulating the stars and involved in the hippy slimeball world, peddling devious political bollocks whilst having a mercenary approach to the punk thing. That being said, Mick got the best out of us, producing a sound that gave credence to our efforts and I feel a substance that has lasted.

Whilst recording there, the singer from Uriah Heep, David Byron, had booked recording time and was staying in the pub. His appearance and his attitude was, well, how can I say ? He had bought the U.S. of A's package before it became mainstream. He had long curly hair, a sun tan, wore jogging clothing and revealing a sun tanned chest decorated with gold chains and medallions. He spoke to me in that rather stilted artistic voice of the difference between the United States of America and the UK. His judgement was heavily influenced by the amount that people could win on game shows. He saw this as a measurement of this country's backwardness, how dim we were and how it explained the low expectations of the people who live in the UK. He told me in excited language of the smallness of people here, whilst, in the States, it seemed they were a wholly satisfied well adjusted species, because of the availability of burgers when you wanted them. He told me of a place where it is easy for a person to become a millionaire, own a tract of land, go on a game show and win a convertible Cadillac and more prize money than people earn in this country for a lifetime's work and it happens everyday. In fact, it is just accepted by people who have this good fortune as an everyday occurrence in a country where people will stop, applaud and congratulate you if you drive by them in a car that they cannot afford themselves and knowing you have a million dollars in your back pocket because they're not jealous like people in the UK. He told me to get in shape. He had just returned from a jog and he was off to the local gym. He went on to tell me how in this country people "don't know their own bodies". This was breakfast time, just him and me in the back room of this pub.

Anyway, Dave Byron left and went over to the studio for the session he had booked, bouncing with the vitality of having a perfectly tuned body and mind. Three hours later I went over to the studio and there was Dave, on his hands and knees, screaming and crying. Apparently, he had just drunk a couple of bottles of brandy and the emotions had become a bit frayed. Poor sod. He died a year or so later, the hedonistic doctrines of self-worship and materialism lost out to the troubled self which had to be saturated with toxic stimulants for it all to be made bearable.

The LP was recorded in two blocks. Finishing the first half, we went off to play some gigs. The Lurkers played quite a few gigs and, as already said, the rougher an area's reputation, the better they seemed to like us. I would say that some of the nastiest places in this country are the supposedly cosy picturesque village *cum* little market towns. They have a dark repressive undertone. When sighting anything different, they want to strike up a posse, get out their ferrets and guns and kill it. We spun around this glorious green land in our van, stopping one afternoon to play in a small pub in Tiverton, a place in Devon; another 'miss booking'. Howard and I went into a couple of the local pubs for a drink before we played. We knew that it was all wrong. We bumped into a few punk fans that had come to see us. They had travelled some distance from towns like Taunton, making their way forty and more miles to see a group and enjoy their time. But, in that kind of situation, I was always anxious for the safety of these people and always for good reason. I noticed in one of the rehabilitative clinics passing itself off as a rustic country pub, the locals. Thirty year old men, who, like many others, self police themselves into a state of being resentful of anything over the walls of their self created prisons. They were staring across at us, nudging one another, grinning, with beady eyes showing maliciousness. Howard and I knew there would be trouble. These churls had smelt their prey. At the gig it was fairly predictable. The young punk fans jumped around in front of the small stage whilst the hill men stood at the back, together, holding their glasses to their chests and grinning inanely, just waiting for one of their herd to stamp his hoof. We were not that long into the gig when one of them felt an atavistic twinge, two of his eight brain cells fused together and did what was natural. They reacted by throwing glasses, kicking out, mouths set in an anger; to my mind far too extreme as it was incited only by the sight of a bunch of skinny, almost children jumping around. Glasses came at us. I swung around one of my cymbal stands, a usual survival response but it was useless. We had to run for it, shielding our heads and diving for cover under the direction of the pub manager into the basement. Whilst under cover, I lost my temper at this, the manager, when he said, "If you've come down from the smoke looking for trouble, then you've found it with our boys." It was hopeless trying to explain to this human advertisement hoarding as it is to many others with similar perceptual insights and sensibilities, that the word is bullying.

The police arrived, having the same sentiment as their half brother, the guv'nor of the tavern who pours them their alcoholic linctus so they can forget what a waste of spunk they are. They told us to, "Drive out of town." I don't believe any of the people who came to see us were seriously hurt on what was yet another lovely outing into the countryside for convivial enjoyment and to experience the British sense of fair play.

Another change in our line up was to occur before recording the second half of our LP. When Kim joined The Lurkers, I thought great, he came from a group that I liked. But he wasn't to be a gregarious fun loving Aussie. In fact, he rarely drank, always had the flu, moaned a lot and didn't think much of me as a drummer. The relationship with him was what I imagined it to be like working in an office. Through his sessions on Lem-Sips, it seemed he was stirring trouble, wanting me out of the group and all that bollocks. You try but some you cannot please. He thought us odd. Pete asked him to leave and Nigel returned. We were learning that it seemed we were seen as a strange bunch, we made others feel uncomfortable as we did not fit into the ordinary mould.

About that time we played a gig in Deptford, organised by some agency having a motivated political agenda. We knew nothing about this kind of thing but I had my thoughts to the angle of many of the people involved in presenting a political point as a front to sell music. I saw it as another system, having defining boundaries of acceptance where one has to adhere to principles. It seemed to me to be an easy ruse for the unscrupulous to hide behind. When watching the personal behaviour of those who set themselves up as being at the vanguard for a particular social topic, the word hypocrisy came to mind and a sentiment of them being using, slimy, devious, sneaky fuckers. In my simple naivety, what always struck me first about these types is that they hardly drank. The glass or bottle is there as a prop but no meaningful drinking was done. And there was that hippy slimeball way of protruding the lower jaw and showing teeth closed together, often accompanied with a silent laugh, the heartfelt shaking and nodding of the head but quickly checking the watch as the mind was scheming further down the line of the project. But, the sign that often alerted me to this type was the fact that they didn't drink. They were not really one of the crowd and in fact they wanted to control it.

The local authority employed those people organising this particular gig. It was an event aimed to heighten awareness to matters affecting people in the community. You could see the points that these people were gaining personally as they schemed and developed their curriculum vitae and portfolio or whatever it's called. All with the ambitions of using what they can to convey themselves up the career ladder. And it did not matter whatever the banner being waved was, whether it was to do with race, employment or sexuality, there they were, the co-ordinators knowing all the answers. Of course, it has seemingly always been the same, the outcast, those on the side, used for whatever purposes to suit the wants of some who will take advantage of the situation.

Not having the advantage of higher or any formal education, nor coming from a background that showed me the ropes around areas and people in the society that I came from, does have disadvantages for many reasons. Yet, there are advantages from having an objective position or being on the outside. To see through the deceit of those who preach with so much arrogance was, at first, seen as stupid, a laugh but then later I was to understand the power of status. To see the 'black person' bracketed as a project. On the one hand, making society aware of the inequities that exist; then to distance their product for it to be clinically marketed and, when finished, to move on to the next project. The CV is all in place but the 'black person' is left in the margin to be used as the other, the devil, in music, politics or whatever, there to be judged and judged by. The 'whitey' liberal is the new 'slave master', constraining with the label, to distinguish, describe and ascribing a personality that does not allow a person's individual personality to come to the fore. But 'white men' have the power to use a double edged sword to liberate and confine. Parts of the black culture are accommodated, thus absorbed into the dominant mainstream. The white accountant now wears a baggy shirt hanging outside his baggy shorts complete with a cap turned back to front, all bought by his children in a family catalogue under 'Leisure Wear'. Once ridiculed and sneered at, the clothing is now acceptable but 'black man' remains outside, left for further use.

Through the years I have come across those who blatantly use people to further their career prospects yet it is the sneakiness of this liberal altruism that narks me. A few years of having an office in a notoriously run down area is vacated for a more pleasant space in the Home Counties. A bit like the vicar having to do his time in a poor parish, then rewarded by being given a middle class environment to save souls who have paid-up mortgages, insurance and personal pension plans. A pseudo white opportunistic middle class using people for selfish purposes, whether it is in local or central government, music or student politics, all leading to one's career path being bettered. Then a structured guilt of giving back to justify positions and privileges. A language is adopted to hide behind but the practices of their own personal life are set aside. The Tory manager type live down the same road as the Liberal/Labour public service professional, hunting for the same school placements, demanding services and taking privileges that perpetuate that very inequity that they create so much verbiage about.

Rant ? Who me ?

No, I took a healthy interest in the things that happened around me, letting it all go over my head, taking from it what I could. Anyway ...

The absurdity and funny side of people marketing human difference and preference for personal profit is evident for everyone to see. From the white public schooler wearing a Rasta hat but keeping his shares options firmly in his back pocket, then years later he talks of his experimental days around the dinner party table to the many others who stand on the platform waiting for a ride at Gravy Train Station.

I remember in 1978 seeing Tom Robinson down the Marquee and good they were as well. But, the hysteria of it all was a bit stupid. The hetro (seemingly) couples held hands whilst singing along to gay anthems that were to become political levers in gaining liberty. A year or so later, John Plain, who joined The Lurkers, reckons he went into a studio one day on his push bike and from nowhere this racy little sports car brushed him aside. It screeches to a halt and out jumps Tom Robinson, accompanied by another racy little number, a good looking young woman *cum* model type. 'Bloody 'ell', John said in his Northern accent, 'I think I'll turn gay meself'.

So it goes.

We played a few more gigs before going back to Worcester to record the second half of our LP. One of the gigs was in Leeds. It was to be Mike Stone's last gig with us, an irony or a coincidence, what with him coming from Leeds and all that.

Recording the second half of our LP with Nigel felt better. I have not met Mick Glossop since those days but I would like to have a chat with him about the recording. Looking back, it seemed at the time that it was the case that 'I didn't have a clue'. I don't know, I just think I would like to meet him. He would most probably think, 'no way, not that neurotic mad person again'.

Still, all the same, Mick's perseverance and insight, I believe, paid off. We were inexperienced and probably hard to reach, out of a mixture of arrogance and stupidity, the latter is likely to be the foremost reason. Mick produced a record which I believe gave us a direction that we should have followed which was to be a bit more obscure and deal with the psychology of our characters, giving the music more room for expressing those feelings and ideas. This was explored through songs like Gerald, a different musical approach accommodating the confused ramblings of a psychopath. Maybe that is where we should have gone, rather than try and compete in the Power Pop culture and worse still, later to play rhythm and blues clichés as emulated by those people with cigarettes sticking out of the corner of their mouths doing cheap talent night impersonations of

The Rolling Stones. As was the case later when 'Honest' John Plain snided his way into the group from playing with The Boys. No, I think given our own natural path we would have developed into something a bit original and I feel Mick saw that but there you are.

The recording was done and The Lurkers were getting some air play. 'Ain't Got A Clue' was Kid Jenson's 'record of the week'. Things were moving along for us. The press became involved in our little world although not as much as some other groups who played to as many people as we did or sold the records that we did. We were rather ignored but then we must have been hard for a young journalist to package. Having no conscious plan, we were seen as idiotic or ignorant and our record company's style of publicity was seen as corny and stupid. In the main, we were packaged by the young journalists as 'Ramone clones', basic, brutish, boastful and bullying. It was never meant that way but so it was. We were often ignored and frequently ridiculed.

Naïve ?

My excuses can be that we were or I was untaught, moving in a world where I was artless, an honesty of responding with spontaneity. I told one of the journalists in an interview, when talking about groups around at that time, that Bodies by the Sex Pistols was brilliant. It was like white blues and Johnny Rotten was Tommy Steel gone mad and that is how I saw Johnny Rotten. He was the 1970's clown and I am sure that is how he saw the whole circus that was created around him. At times I should have thought more than I spoke but my intentions were usually friendly. We were suspicious all the same of those in the media and their purposes. Sometimes our suspicions were realised when reading once that a journalist had let the tape on which he had recorded an interview with us to play in his office for the amusement of his peers and then described us as the 'most inarticulate bunch of bozos'. This attitude and the values by these middle class journalist types of people having to be intelligent fuelled my prejudices. They were coming on like all those BBC quiz programmes that I watched as a child. The opposing families, with father who knows best and the look on the face of a child when seeing his father exposed for not being as intelligent as the other father. It's the competitive culture and there they were, working in rock 'n' roll, 'man'. Bringing along with them the point scoring card of, 'who is intelligent ?' Which one of the groups is 'top of the form ?'

That's how I saw it.

There they were again, the white middle class standing in judgement, still aiming to impress father after doing their homework. However, all being said, some of the things that I did say, well, I should not have. I was always drunk, rambling confused words and feelings and what I would have considered as humour did not translate. The literal misunderstanding and a conscious detachment by the young journalists in order to say what they are not, became a routine and habit. There was the selectivity to sell an image and make a story by the journalists but uncaring thugs we were not. It comes again to a cultural understanding of what fits in with the sway of fashion having its parameters of acceptance and values set firmly in place. The pressure from peers to conform, aspiring to be seen as a certain type, even an accent or culturally judged physical deficit conjures up a fear. By making flippant remarks and hiding behind grinning humour could and should be easy to unmask but it was amplified by the journalists and, where not existing, it was constructed. Were we seen to be boastful of our outsider status ? If we were, it should have been obvious why. There were journalists who did like us and supported us and I think for that reason.

The typical student writer came from the NME, a place to develop the CV and springboard one's career. One in particular was Paul Morley who came to review one of our gigs. I thought I was being friendly when I met him, offered him a drink and tried to make him feel welcome but he would not let anything like that infringe on his essay with its content of us as ignorant and rude. Obviously he didn't fancy me and he had already bracketed us into whatever it was that had been shaped by his predetermined assumptions. All things considered, it would be fair to say that any little bit of publicity that did come our way, I would open my big mouth and that would go towards ruining it. In one of the interviews, I accused members of groups like The Clash and The Damned of doing anything to further their career. I said things like them being posers and throwing their grandmothers down the escalators if it fitted the publicity angle. It seemed arty school stuff, the Clash staring at the camera, conscious of every minute detail to create the correct presentation, choreographed dance steps whilst laying down the music for class revolution dressed in chic fatigues having that all important label.

It was a bit of a shame really, as I saw the Clash in their very early days and thought they brilliant but liking the energy was one thing, buying the designer revolutionary look fresh from the 'Ents' committee of a student union was another. After I made this criticism in the article, we got a message from the group asking us to come and meet them at their rehearsals in Fulham. I popped down there but I'm a different sort of person from what they are. They were heading for Hollywood or somewhere even if they professed to 'be bored with the USA'. I don't know and good luck to them but cut the patronising class shit when it is obviously a marketing vehicle. The group, roadies and hangers on were in acceptable uniform, a kind of mix and match punk/grunge/squat ex-hippie type of look. And then we walk in, the suburban gimps, coming down for a chat, about what and having what relevance, fuck knows. Mick Jones, the guitarist, spoke to me about us 'all having the same goals'. 'Career Opportunities'. Yeah, 'sure man'.

The Lurkers went on their cultural route, free from the advice of fashion designers and the spectre of having disadvantages because of one's private school education. One of our supporters tried to get Fulham Football Club to play a few tracks from our LP, Fulham Fallout but they would not entertain the idea. It was the 'punk thing' I suppose and the chap playing the discs down there at that time did sound a bit plummy in the voice region. I thought that maybe he had fallen from grace, letting down his titled family and all that, so someone got him a 'little job' down at Fulham Football Club, spinning a few discs and making announcements with a nuance of sarcasm. But then it was most probably nothing to do with it at all.

I always held the club in such lofty regard which could go back to my childhood of being bullied by my older brother to watch and support Fulham and him influencing me that all comments made by people down at the ground were out of my conceptual thinking range and that the place was falling apart with the amount of intellectuals stuffed in and around it. I grew to have this snobbery when considering other teams and my mad brother Douglas would add the meanings himself to comments made by the announcer at half time, the 'fallen man from the City,' about opposing fans, especially if they had travelled down from 'up north'. There was sneering and searing digs that were pitched beautifully ten miles above the heads of the Northerner's heads so that we could chuckle as we were privy to this feast of wit and thrown away genius – no wonder a lot of the Northerners think the Southerners are a stuck up bunch.

However, the person who was asked if it would be alright to play tracks off the LP said no. I must admit that I did feel let down really. It is because I felt this closeness with the name Fulham Football Cub. I hardly went at that time but that did not matter. It was the place my dad and his family came from and of course my surname, Haynes. There was Johnny Haynes, the legendary Fulham player. I caught the end of his playing days down at Fulham, being taken by my brother Douglas and occasionally his friend Robby, who was a Scotsman, came along. They would sometimes stop at a pub, bring out light and bitter and a soft drink for me being just eight or nine years of age. I remember on one of those Saturdays a needy tramp asked Robby if he had 'sixpence for a cup of tea'. "I was just about to ask you the same question," Robby replied to him, in a polite, clear and concise eastern Scottish accent. Douglas winked at me, reassuring me that everything was under control and that everybody connected with the Fulham experience were two steps ahead of everybody else.

Anyway, yes, Johnny Haynes, captained England for five years and was 'the first one hundred pound a week footballer', also 'the greatest passer of the ball the game has ever seen'. Now, my dad says that Johnny Haynes was his dad's cousin's son. Allegedly, my Uncle Frank spoke to him a number of times when he bumped into him in the Fulham area. Although my mum says there is a question mark over all this. As a child I was a member of the club, not a season ticket holder, just a member. They sent me a card and a badge but also raffle tickets to sell at Christmas time.

"Who are they ?" people would sneer jokingly on their doorstep as I trudged the local area, nervous at the prospect of not selling my quota. I was about eleven years old at the time. In the back of my mind, there being guilt as I thought of those Chelsea and West Ham Typhoo Tea cards under my bed.

This contributed to the feeling I had with Fulham Football Club, at a young age developing a self-effacing irony by being associated with the underdog. And all those years later, for them not to play our record over their tannoy. Apparently, the response to the request to play it was, "It's not really our thing." It seemed Fulham FC was not ready for punk rock. It was three years after their appearance at Wembley, playing West Ham in the FA Cup with the legendary display by the Fulham goalie Peter Mellor underpinning Fulham's 2-0 defeat. I remember on the day of the match they had a run down of the player's interests in the papers, their tastes in music and hobbies. Most of them reeled out the predicable stuff, Rod Stewart, Disco's, steak and chips, golf, going for a meal with wife/girlfriend and there was a photograph of Peter Mellor in the kitchen, doing what he did best to relax, cooking. He was wearing a pinnie rather than overalls or kitchen whites or whatever they're called, smiling and showing a cake he had just baked. Maybe it all fitted in, they not wanting to associate with anything so vile as punk rock groups as they considered themselves too lofty and civilised.

Anyway, there has been full redemption in recent years with Al Fayed parading Michael Jackson around the ground, holding a parasol *cum* umbrella over the gloved one's head. In addition, the Fulham faithful smiled at him as he walked gingerly in the drizzle at the side of London's version of the Ganges. Old Father Thames must have thought, 'I thought I had seen it all'. And the Fulham grateful clapped readily at this spectacle, like condemned men would smile readily at anyone who might save them from a certain death. However, as I write, the mighty whites are now in the Premier League. Let's see what occurs.

It was June 1978, we were due to do our record of the week 'Ain't Got A Clue' on Top Of The Pops but the luck of The Lurkers struck on cue. Scotland was in the world cup and they were playing that night so they dropped the show. It was a shame for us as it was our biggest selling record but to make it up to us we were told that they would fit us in at a later date. Although our television exposure was not to be held back, a couple of weeks later we went on Revolver, a good music show hosted by Peter Cook. The show was produced by Micky Most. I spoke to him in the bar or canteen, most probably boring him or irritating him, going on about the different snare drum sounds he got on those massive selling pop records that he had produced. He smoked a large cigar, striking me as a hard person, bit gangsterish, telling me about his 'Roller'. I think he might have thought I was a young punk with a grievance so he could have been a bit on the defensive but I just wanted to know what recording The Animals and Mud was like.

One of our managers, Nick Austin, was at the recording of the show. I am not sure what relationship I had with Nick or Martin Mills come to that. I suppose they were a bit like prefects at school, the older boys who knew best and we were the callow boys. I have always made the mistake in my life of thinking well of someone if they smiled at me when I spoke to or ranted at them and Nick and Martin would smile but I didn't know them well. Nick would invariably annoy people wherever he went, making unoriginal comments and having that particular personality that many people find very irritating. He was running around the studio in his Tesco bomber jeans with six inch turn ups, giving orders and making demands on things he had no knowledge of or skills in but, regardless of that, he just went on intruding uninvited. I was told that Micky Most told him to get out of the Director's Box after imparting his great wisdom, telling Micky Most what camera angles were needed and giving directions to where he should make changes. His embarrassing escapades went unnoticed to himself, of course but people did approach us at various places and ask if he was really our manager and, when given the answer, saying 'why ?' Micky Most wasn't impressed but Nick soldiered on in his gimpy way making his comments, seemingly unaware of his actions but then he did sign us up, so in part it is explained.

Anyhow, with Nick banned from the 'box', we did our thing and hung around for hours. I shook hands with Peter Cook and for some reason was amazed at how tall he was. He seemed like a judge or something, maybe he was. But as with all our experiences, The Lurkers were not that good at mixing with the 'in' crowd. I remember the night being marred when Howard's bloody girlfriend stole beer from my bag which put me in a very bad mood and I ended up talking to this bloke who was a scene shifter and total bullshitter.

The show was recorded in Birmingham; the same studio where Crossroads was made. I was not a Crossroads fan so I wasn't that impressed with the tales this chap was telling me of who he knew and who he had worked with. He seemed to have a drink problem and told me in his Brummie tone of the times he had put Noel Gordon to rights, she who played the character Meg Richardson in the show Crossroads. He told me a story of him presenting a bouquet of flowers to her when she arrived at the studio one morning as a 'wind up' and everyone was laughing behind her back. This bloke was like many that I've met in this area of work. He was resentful and probably a creep who crawled around those that he criticised and got even only in the imaginary events he lied about. He went on to tell me how untalented these actors were and then going into detailed descriptions of how to carry a large board or a heavy piece of wood. He told me that I would learn about the game if I stuck at it. He could tell I didn't wear any make up when we did our recording, going on to tell me that he knows the blokes in the make up game, "just a bit of powder, not the full queer works." But these were things that I would learn. The bar was shutting, I was bored senseless and it was a 105 miles drive back to London.

I thought about it all, this chap in the bar, what I was doing and how things were working out for us as a group. I wasn't inspired by anything; our neuroses had not changed. Neither Howard, Pete or myself could drive, I was twenty two years old and I still considered it an adult thing to do, done by others. On the way home I sat in the back of the van, thinking I would like to smack Howard's girlfriend in the mouth for stealing drink from my bag and with the image of Nick Austin in my mind, making him and us look like fools. At times he might have meant well but he had an approach that wasn't engaging to certain people. It could well have been something to do with his school background, I don't know but he certainly rubbed people up the wrong way. Archetypal behaviour of his was demonstrated in an Earls Court pub just down the road from where Beggar's Banquet had their offices at that time. This pub, which I went in only a few times, was a place used by mercenaries. I don't mean the ones coming from the music business but the hired killer types, the Soldiers of Fortune. They would chalk up on a board the going rate and destinations, the fees and places on this beautiful Earth where work could be found. At that time, it was Angola I remember. The place was rough, used predominately by white South Africans, Australians and a few Scottish. It was rowdy and to even the most least perceptive person it was a place to mind one's self in the company of these desperately unhappy men. Yet, this obvious fact was lost on Nick Austin, lacking the diplomacy, awareness and seemingly the sense for self survival, he elbowed his way to the bar one evening. I wasn't there. The scene was witnessed by Plug (Pete Edwards). An eight foot South African took a dislike to Nick's bad manners and cautioned him over the matter. Nick took no notice, gave him a look of indifference and continued to hold his note out to be served but he held it out for just a few seconds before this chap had held his personal court of judgement and acted out the sentence which was to deliver a head butt to Nick that knocked him out.

For a while after Nick ran around with a sticky plaster cross on the bridge of his nose that had been badly broken. Still, Nick went about his way, seemingly uncaring, with his pride untouched which was more than could be said for Scotland's football team. Their involvement in the World Cup, which they so selfishly got themselves qualified into so that we missed our opportunity of going on Top Of The Pops, was over. They were beaten, so not making the final in which Argentina beat Holland 3-1. Four years later, we were to be at war with them, meaning Argentina; 'we' - 'them'.

The BBC were true to their word. In August, we went into a studio and recorded 'I Don't Need To Tell Her' which we would mime over the following day in a television studio for Top of the Pops. The studios are not a great distance from where we live so it was a quick drive down the Western Avenue, get the okay at the gate, collect our passes and then hang around all day. I remember thinking that, for such an influential institution, the studio was a very modest place and the BBC had the atmosphere of a school. The smell of the polished corridors, the aching faces of the women clerical staff clutching their bits of paper and giving sniffy looks; the place seemed distanced from the general malaise of the everyday world having its own feeling of quietude. It is the kind of thing a person would hate and recoil from or grow to rely on, connect with and spend all their life at.

The coincidence I mentioned earlier of the part that DJ Dave Lee Travis played in my punk journey was that he was the presenter on the day we did the show. I thought to myself, 'should I tell him about what I thought all those years ago whilst in my room at home with him going on about Demis Roussos ?' Except it wasn't really that long ago but it seemed years. Maybe for him nothing had changed, just another wave of fashion that he and his agent will accommodate. Long hair, spiky hair, glittered face, no face, sandalled feet, platform soles, quiet song, loud song, jump about, stand still and so it goes; all in a days work for a pro. I did not want to lay the blame for the world's iniquities upon him as was often the way of those trying to get inside of the power bases. No, I saw people like him for what they are, doing a job, perpetuating the status quo, yes but one that I could not get passionate about. So there was no thrusting my finger in his face and levelling a blistering volley of vitriol about class war as many a punk would be expected to do. And it was funny in a way, during the afternoon I got into a lift, the doors closed, I turned around and there he was standing next to me. I didn't tell him about all the feelings I had at that time but I did say that I remembered him playing Demis Roussos and the part it played in shaping my musical direction. He went on to tell me that it is the 'powers that be', it was them that were making him play this crap and we have to get through to them before we can play anything decent or anything can change, etcetera. I nodded and looked closely at him. He was a big man, as I expected, maybe greedy but he was as I thought. The lift doors opened, he exited and I felt a loop or something had been completed.

During late afternoon, the rehearsals took place; ours consisted of a quick run through. The group Child was on the show, one of the boy bands of their day. They had this pretty boy image. I didn't speak to them but they seemed pleasant enough. I nodded to a couple of them as they looked on with a bit of embarrassment as their sleazy looking manager bloke was standing a full eight inches from the singer's face, giving him last minute instructions, checking the thickness of his make up, pulling in a make up person to add final points of perfection. I pondered, 'Did that bloke who worked in the Crossroads studio know of this particular technique ?' I got a nod from one of the group that said, 'yeah, we know', as the manager fussed over his 'principal boy'. 'Mm', I thought to myself, my moans of self irony could never match what these chaps were putting themselves through.

Child practised their moves and we retired to the bar; it was Plug's (Pete Edwards) birthday but the day was very low key. Sham 69, who we knew, were doing the show and some of their roadies and fans were there. Most of them were intent to dislike their surroundings. It was like a factory outing for them and not much fun. They seemed to take comfort in their own self-repression. Evening came and the show was recorded under the fastidious orders of a fay stage manager. I had this feeling Child were going to have preference over us when it came to the soft focus. Sham did their hit 'When The Kids Are United'. Jimmy Purcey was having difficulty explaining to the floor manager of the significance of wanting one of the followers of his group to come on stage at the beginning of the song, on cue the two of them shake hands and Jimmy says '"Ello mate," etc and then go into the song. Jimmy's frenetic, bedlam-like behaviour was trying the nerves of the Stage Manager. Anyhow, we did our turn. We were fairly drunk. I was told to stop messing around by one of the obsequious prefects on orders from he, the Stage Manager. The Liverpudlian soul group, The Real Thing was on the show. During our recording, the singer stood behind one of the speakers making jokes with me. I had taken off my jacket and flung it over a speaker cabinet. He was mucking around with it and this didn't go down too well. When everyone had done their bit, we were told that Sham 69 and ourselves had to do it again. There was a bit of a problem as nearly all the audience had gone except for a few stragglers. There were no autograph hunters at this gig baby. We were told the Stage Manager was furious. So, we recorded it again, Jimmy getting this bloke to shake his hand before going into the song and then us except we couldn't stop buggering about. The scene became a little absurd. There were only about eight bored young people left in the place so the Stage Manager sent his assistant off to retrieve some unsuspecting souls to return. Most of them were Shepherd's Bush's finest, young bored looking girls wearing ridiculous party dresses. This being before the days of bringing in aspiring dancers and actresses who are trained in dance and dress to accompany the image of the groups on the show. Yes, these were the days of the vacuous, gum-chewing youngsters, liking hardly anything but it was something to tell friends at school about the next day.

They shot the action in angles that gave the impression that the place was jumping with vibrant young things getting giddy, in that BBC style and all under the power of him, the Stage Manager. The sensibilities of the Stage Manager had been teased and stretched too far. I remember him saying something like, "It's finished", "whatever", "never before", "this is unprofessional". He wasn't pleased but it had to do and, as for us, we were off to play in places where the antics and professional approach would make Mr Stage Manager swing his handbag in total rage.

For some reason, during the group's travels, Bradford became a favourite of mine. It was a place where I saw and met some good characters, grim but good, just like the physical environment where the town finds itself. I suppose us being 'Southern snobs' loaded with preconceived ideas of 'Northerners' and their ways had something to do with it. The names of the places around there made up my liking for a world that was probably mythical and possibly inspired by my childhood memories of Kent Walton on Saturday afternoons. He would present the wrestling, inviting me to that Halifax Baths or Dewsbury Town Hall. I would imagine the smell of chip shops, the mist from the moors, a foreboding place and sadly home to a seemingly disproportionate amount of notorious murderers. The mood had been set by the distant whining tone of

Eddie Waring with his earthy descriptions of a life and culture. It was a place where I pieced together a fabric that most likely would not be recognised by people who actually come from the place.

However, so it was, I travelled armed with prejudices, memories and some kind of psychological wanting to belong and identify to a place I didn't know but had only conjured up from illusory images. It was not the decadence and Day Glow wrappings of New York City for what interested me was the grim reality, chip wrappings and a madness, occupied by a people who, through their dour loneliness, maybe held the essence of the spirit of the 'other'. We drove to Bradford, taking the M1, then the M6 and after finding the pub that we were playing at in the town, we went about getting the gear into the place. I forget the name of the pub; it was something like The Royal Standard. Anyway, this bloke came out of the pub and stood on the pavement next to me. He maintained a fixed stare at me as I was lumping the gear through the doors. I said something like, "You alright mate ?" I felt I should say something as he was staring right at me. A pale smile opened in his face but his eyes continued to stare. "Oh aye, oh aye, I'm alright, don't bloody worry about that," he said in his Bradford tone. He followed me into the pub and asked who I was. I told him that I was the drummer. "Fuck off," he said, telling me I was too fat and ugly and the wrong shape, it didn't look right to him, seeing me as a drummer and all that. No, I had to be the bouncer. He stood square on in front of me. He was in his thirties, a big bloke, wearing a white T-shirt and old fashioned wrist straps that strong men from a past era would wear.

I looked around the bar, it looked quite ordinary for this type of small gig, a tiny stage, sticky carpet and a couple of bored barmaids preparing things for when it opened. I noticed that around the walls were black and white photographs of British wrestlers, some were signed. I looked at him. His eyes had been following mine with an insane smile and a nod that acknowledged that I had noticed the photographs. He said "That's right, oh yeah, oh fucking yes, mate." Holding out his hand he said, "Shake." I knew he was going to crush my hand. Cautiously, I held mine towards his. He grabbed at it and squeezed. I gasped immediately, he was happy. "Me name's Malcolm Fairplay, fair play by name and fair play by nature. Got yer there, didn't I, yer soft Southern bastard." Holding my hand and standing side on, I grinned at him. He said, "You're alright you are." Putting his arm around my shoulders, he directed me to the bar. "C'mon, you daft Southern cunt, I'll get yer a drink and I bet you want that piss all you queers drink down there, aye, aye, I know, bloody lager."

He told me we could get a drink even though the pub wasn't open because

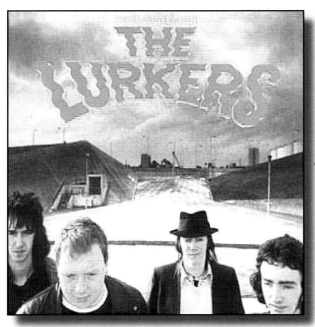

*That awful cover
for our LP
'God's Lonely Men'*

Arturo, Howard, me & Pete Stride – 'look moody boys'

'The Fulham Crowd'
Lee, Eddie, ? (sorry), Max, Bully

Outside a studio in Southall where we recorded the 7 inch
blue vinyl record 'Chelsea's Gonna Win'.
Mark Wyeth, me, Paul Fox.

A gig in the early days.
That chap's name is Fred in the centre of the photo.

There we are.

Marquee

less £20 → roadies
£3 → kebab
£15 - taxi -Wall.

RDOUR STREET, LONDON W.1.   TEL: 01-437-6603

40 2405 17

ce Club Box Office on ....Monday 9th February

Re: Your Guest List

)273	- 49843	£ 712 : 50	p
)542	- 12572	£ 33 : 00	p
7249	- 32296	£ 47 : 00	p

Gross includes V.A.T. £ 792 : 50

Less V.A.T. £ 58 : 70

r Percentage purposes £ 733 : 80

ntage.. (70 %) ......£ 513 : 66

lit Commission (5%) ..£ 25 : 68

THE V.A.T. OF THE ABOVE FEE RECEIVED, I.E. £ 41.09 WILL
BE PAID BY THIS OFFICE ONLY UPON RECEIPT OF YOUR COMPANY'S
OFFICIAL INVOICE SHOWING YOUR REGISTERED V.A.T. NUMBER.

513-66
LESS   25-68 AGENCY FEE
487.98
less The Vipers 50.00
437.98
less The Brest 25.00
412.98

MANAGER-MARQUEE CLUB

A receipt from the Marquee Club that was in Wardour Street,
Soho in London. Attached is a note of extra amounts
deducted from what we were paid; £20 for 'roadies,' £3 for a
kebab and £15 for a taxi to take Howard home.
I didn't know that he got a taxi — and who had the kebab?

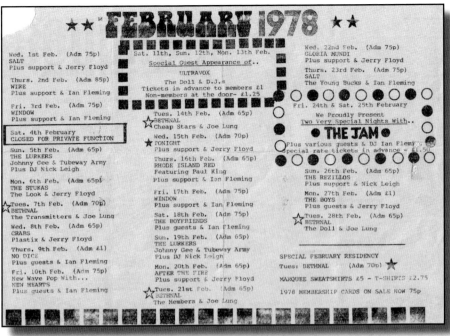

The Marquee gig guide.
God knows how long Jerry Floyd was the DJ down there.

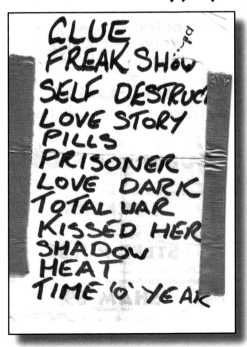

Our set list.

A photograph with Kim Bradshaw, and Plug (Pete Edwards) poking his head into the shot with The Sun newspaper in his pocket; I wonder if he's finished the crossword yet ?

In some service station somewhere.

A publicity photograph for our 'gold disc'.

The Lurkers

Beggar's Banquet

'Hold the pose boys'

ESSO grips Soundsman in friendly stranglehold, Howard Wall looks on

Pic by Paul Slattery

Luck of the Lurkers?

THEY TOLD us that everything would be laid on. Every whim of our journalistic fancy would be catered for, and we were fooled. The coaches laid on for The Lurkers' opening gig on their forthcoming tour pulled slowly away from Beggar's Banquet's Fulham shop at 7 o'clock on Friday evening, an hour later than scheduled.

The drinking had started two or three hours earlier. Bushell was well gone, slobbering in that macho way he's perfected, signing autographs and kissing kiddies wearing 'I discovered Howard Wall' tee shirts. Me? I was stone deadly sober. I was on a diet. I felt like a crocodile in a handbag factory by the time we were creeping out of London (the coach driver appeared as drunk as the rest of the mob), stopping outside a surburban pub for a much requested, obviously much needed slash.

We stopped (and this is an accurate count from a seriously sober mind)? more times before reaching Peterborough. From what I can remember these 'sessions' consisted of half naked kids scampering drunkenly to the nearest grass verge along the motorway, swinging half full cans of Heineken before watering the grass, while a stoned Paul Slattery, alleged photographer, cried "Keep it up, squire . . . ah, nice one!".

Meanwhile on the coach, the beer continued to swill, stale salami sandwiches were thrown merrily at passing cars, as Bushell and yours truly became the theme of several football songs from these Lurker thugs, myself receiving the brunt of the abuse at the hands of what appeared to be an eight year old vole who took a special delight in poking me in the chest with a Lurkers poster and seeing if I'd float in a largish pool in which my feet paddled.

It was ten o'clock when we arrived in Peterborough, feeling much the same I'd guess as Man Utd must have felt when they watched Arsenal's third goal being tucked away at Wembley. But it wasn't long before One Of My Favourite Bands trod shyly into the Peterborough Ravina's blazing spotlight, and it wasn't very long (a handful of songs, sadly) before they marched reluctantly off the same stage, gang-busted into cancelling their first gig for some time in a violent shambles caused irrefutably by the self-same local skins that left a Buzzcocks gig in tatters two weeks previous.

Me? I was thinking about the kid who wrote a letter to Sounds ages ago after being done over at the Lurker's Lyceum gig of yore. Peterborough was the first gig he'd been to since, and he'd just been battered about the head by local cops in a battered up old van outside. The luck of The Lurkers? Don't you believe it.

"Why?" was the question that bounced around backstage afterwards. Esso stood like a professional wrestler asking "Why can't we do something?"

But it was all over. The magical mystery Lurks trip was trundling untidily to a close. I looked for Bushell and other friends in the crowd. I couldn't see them. Figures punched wildly at each other, blood trickled across grim faces.

As I left Peterborough kids were nearly in tears, pleading with the band to come back. It was the same few nutters every week, they insisted.

"Last week a kid pulled a knife on me at Brunel . . . " Someone (I think it was Slattery) said, "What are we gonna do about this violence at gigs?" Nobody in the coach could find an answer to that one.

DAVE McCULLOUGH

That's me trying to communicate with Dave McCullough of Sounds.

he was the boss so there was no need to worry as everybody did what he tells them to do. The girls behind the bar smiled with wariness more than sharing Malcolm's fun as he pointed out their physical failings. "Keep 'em on their bloody toes." He turned to me. "Got to, oh yeah, ruined better men than you an' me old cocker." They smiled at him. I was thinking surely there wasn't that much of a job shortage up north. He was pleased as he told me, "You bastards 'ave got a big following round 'ere mate. 'Ad loads of 'em in this afternoon asking if yer playing. Anyway, some of 'em look like right silly bastards 'an all; 'ere, 'ow do you get on with all that, the way they dress 'an all ?" Looking around the place, it was obvious that this was another of our 'miss-bookings'. We had a bit of a name and by what Malcolm was saying, followers of our type of music seemed surprised that we were playing there. There must have been another place in Bradford where the groups who visited played but it was a mystery to us where it was. Malcolm told me that he saw me looking at the photographs on the walls of the British wrestlers. "My friends, a lot of 'em are." He leant close to me, in confidence, telling me that he had been 'involved' himself but quick to add only on an amateur basis. He showed me the photos. I recognised many of them and in a wandering kind of way, I told him of what the North conjured up in my mind. I told him of watching the wrestling as a child, sharing with him the images and feelings of my imagination, something people have told me is a major fault of mine but did it really matter ? After all, I had entered the world of Malcolm Fairplay.

The place was packed. I was drunk. Malcolm took me downstairs to the cellar and proudly showed me the different barrels of beer he had in stock. We were standing amongst these support bars, I was very aware that there was a need for some serious structural building work. They were steel poles fixed from the floor to the ceiling, which was the pub floor upstairs. It was packed with people and the floor was bouncing around dangerously. I asked him if he thought it was safe and what about the law, safety and all that. The floor of the pub was moving up and down about a foot and we were a few inches below it. "Nah, don't worry about it," he said and continuing in a quite and reflective tone he looked at the moving floor. "Who cares; like chickens really, what if they die ? Would it really matter ? Would anyone really give a fuck ?"

Being a bit on the edgy side, I decided it best to go upstairs. Malcolm showed me more of the photos on the walls. There was Jim Breaks, Bert Royal and Vic Faulkner, Alan Dennison 'strong bastard', Les Kellet, Geof Ports the British heavy weight champion. Malcolm told me Geoff had jumped behind the bar at times. Looking at Malcolm, I thought, 'I like the guy.' What it said about me, God knows. By now, I was drunk and raged about the 'Bradford mind'.

He encouraged me in a kind of collusion in building this image. He told me that he would go into some pubs in the town and try to find the ex-wrestler Jim Brakes, telling me that he knew where he might be. Malcolm headed off. Some people who had come to see us asked me about the group but I went on about how I liked Bradford lunacy and that Malcolm was off to find Jim Brakes; our conversations did not last. Malcolm returned, alas, without the great man but I think the gig went well.

There was the post gig atmosphere of a slow weariness as the last remnants of life, seemingly after a battle, drags itself along. There was the pain of getting the gear back in the van and the bar staff went about checking the damage that had been done to the pub and there were the last few remaining people who were lost without means of getting home or too drunk to get home and maybe broken hearted because their supposed loved one had gone home with someone else and of course there were those who did not have a home to go to. There were concerns for last buses and trains, a last minute desperate squeeze with her or him that will be regretted as it should have been done earlier or shouldn't have been done at all. There were the last door promises or curses and the nighttime wind from those unforgiving Moorlands rung its own bell on another night of love, strife and enjoyment. The doors shut and Malcolm Fairplay was in control.

We decided to go for a curry. Malcolm knew the people who ran and worked in the Indian restaurant. He gave the orders and laid the plan for how it all should be. These were the days of the Yorkshire Ripper; this came into our conversation. A couple of the barmaids came with us and Malcolm remarked on one of women's hair, it was dyed blond. He told me it would be brunette next week if the next victim of the Ripper is a blond. The women of Bradford changed their hair colour the opposite to the last woman who had been murdered. Malcolm 'joked' with the woman, holding his knife towards her, telling her that the Ripper is gonna get her. I sat there and thought of the faces of those women who had been killed. There had been many by this time, their faces shown in the newspapers, staring forward, small grainy photographs, some looking as if they came from a dark and distant past where all life was seemingly a grim black and white. I remember thinking of some of the faces. They were faces of people who were destined to live a miserably hard life, scared and brutalised. And then for it all to end in that way.

It came to my mind that a person is kind of sanctioned to kill poor prostitutes. The women offered their life for whatever reason but giving all that they had and to lose that very thing. And those in the normal world will let it spin along with a brief hand on heart and a nod but to conclude with words of pragmatism, saying 'that's life'. Yet, 'that life' means something very different if one of the victims turns out to be a young student as one did. She was attractive, intelligent and had things to live for, it must have been a mistake but now the Ripper had come into being rather than residing in the margins of the consciousness of those who live in the normal world. The people in that place on that night were dealing with all this. To those detached from that environment, Malcolm's humour would be seen as callous and crude but they would be missing the point because it was to those people in that place and maybe even on that night that the horror of another attack could happen. It was their reality and it was how they lived with it. I thought about Malcolm. He too was scared and, like many men in that area, the police might have questioned him.

Tension filled those cramped streets and the minds of all those living there and they had to cope with having to live their lives together and maintain a semblance of ordinary life whilst the pressure rose as everyone was involved and existing under the heavy mood of circumspection, suspicion and fear. I saw Malcolm as a good person. In an age of clever and evasive political language, Malcolm would incite the most negative terminology. But those people are not honest. I knew that those young women felt safe, at least for one evening, and it was because Malcolm was there.

The people that I met whilst we plodded into towns confirmed the ideas that I had about Lurker people. I wrote only a couple of songs, well, the words, and they weren't about whisky and women or political anthems. One was about isolation and avoiding the aggression and confrontation in life. It's called 'It's Quiet Here' and the other was about an attractive young girl who went mad. This was pretty much Lurker material, songs about people who are deemed unsuccessful in the society that they find themselves, being different and often alone and, of course, having no connection with the cool people.

Bridgend in South Wales is a place that I would travel through on a coach when being a child. My annual holiday was to go down to my nan's in South Wales. The place we were playing was, of course, another 'miss-booking' and I always found South Wales to be a grim place to play. We set up the stuff and I went for a bag of chips and a walk around the town. As I was looking in the window of a gentlemen's outfitters, the type that only seem to exist in the provinces, a voice caused me to break from my idle staring at waistcoats and braces. "Alright then, are you ?" I turned and saw this chap standing there, looking at me, well, staring really, he was a couple of years older than me I suppose. "Yeah, not bad mate, thanks," I said to him. He looked me up and down with a mixture of suspicion and excitement. I instantly felt that there might be something up and became tense. He said, "From the smoke are ya ? Same as meself, like." His false cockney accent was absurd, especially as he had spoken in his native Welsh accent a few seconds earlier. "Oh, is that it right ?" I said to him and asked where it was that he came from in London. It was nonsense but I was looking for an escape route. He had scars on his face and I could sense something disturbed lurking inside this poor bloke's being. He continued to talk in his cockney accent. I told him that I played in a group and also told him where we were playing and if he was doing nothing he could come along. He went on about knowing people in the music business who came from down in the 'smoke' and that he could drink more than I could. I told that I was going for a drink in a pub as he followed me down the high street and then he followed me into a pub. I couldn't get rid of him and I noticed that I was getting looks from people in the pub although I would expect some, having cropped hair and a London accent but I felt the looks had an extra bite to them.

He had only taken a sip of his beer and his demeanour changed. Gone was 'cockney geezer out on the beer' and in was the self that was him, a scared young man looking around himself at surroundings and people that made him uneasy. He told me that he wasn't well. "I'm ill, actually," he said in his native Welsh accent. His shoulders sagged and he became nervous. He told me that he felt sick and that he wanted to go to the toilet. He asked if it was alright for him to go. I said it was, trying to adopt a calm bearing of a man in control and off he went to the toilet. The masquerade now gone, he was back to being that anxious, jumbled and uncomfortable person that he probably hated. After a very short time, he returned, asking me if it was okay for him to leave and go home as he didn't feel well. He told me that he took tablets and the drink doesn't mix well with them. I nodded and shook his hand, telling him that of course he can go home and he left, walking in that self-conscious way that people have when they know that they don't and will never, 'fit in'. One of the blokes in the pub came over and spoke to me, telling me that the person I came in with was a patient from the local hospital for 'nutters'. He went on to tell me that they used to be made to wear little yellow badges, to let people know who they were and where they came from. The man who was telling me this laughed, his beaming face fit to burst at the amusement of it all and those standing behind him nodded support at what he was saying. I looked down at the drink that was left standing on the bar. He had taken just a sip. I then looked at the space in the doorway, at the place where one of God's Lonely Men had just walked through. 'Yellow Badge Men,' I thought; it should be the name of our next LP.

This was The Lurkers on tour and wherever we went at least a couple of familiar faces would be there. It might have been the Isle of Arran or even New York and they often made us feel guilty if they couldn't get in to see us, get home or a find a place to stay. There was the Fulham Crowd with Max and Eddie, Steve, Searn and the rest of them; there was Mark, Walt, Perry and others, making their way down to support and belong.

One Saturday in late summer we were in St Austell down in Cornwall. It had been arranged for us to stay in a pleasant old Guest House situated in quaint rustic settings. On arriving there, they seemed a bit concerned about us staying but relaxed after having a chat, telling us that there would be a party taking place that evening and that we would be welcome to attend as we were guests. The gig was a large place, set on the beach and, because it being a holiday resort, there were people from different places and having different tastes. It was packed. There were some blokes from the area we came from down there. They weren't really interested in the punk thing as they were more disco in their manner and would be up for a fight if the occasion arose. Some of the Fulham crowd had made it down but, in the main, it was ostensibly the domain of the straight-back, self repressed fraternity, out to enjoy themselves.

The gig was going quite well, the crowd were pretty active but the atmosphere had a foreign flavour as many in the crowd were playing at punking it up. The place had employed these greaser types as stage bouncers or security or they took it upon themselves to employ themselves. Like a lot of this type, the Rolling Stones concert gave the biker culture this kind of identity. Most of the characters there that night were not the weekend Hells Angels, posing around with ten A levels in Nuclear physics in their back pocket. No, these were your traditional country bumpkin sort of blokes, sturdily built with a sense of humour which goes something like, 'My gun didn't work when I went to shoot a rabbit; what a waste of what could have been a beautiful few seconds of my life,' anyway, something like that. Our followers from Fulham were in the crowd at the front. It was a high stage and the heads of people at the front of the stage were just above the floor of it. Every time some of the crowd clambered up on to the stage for a dance around, these biker churls would bundle them off and none too friendly like. They started to get nasty and as I said peoples' heads were bobbing just above the floor at the foot of the stage and these bouncers started kicking out and connecting in the faces of some people. A few of the crowd were drawing this to our attention. Howard started having a moan at them but the bikers from imbecile world thought it a joke as they were physically bigger than everyone else and they had been given a bit of power which to many of their type, having the developed personality of a snot ridden tissue as used by a long term patient at Broadmoor, a feeling of power and having some control in their deficient lives is a dangerous thing.

I always had a problem with bouncers or, let's say, these types who found a stage to expel their vicious streak and often in a cowardly manner. There were many nights when I would get upset and frustrated by some of these people. I remember being severely threatened as I was warned to back off because I had a go at this member of security at Brunel University. This member of the security was on the stage hitting out at members of the crowd wearing a thick ring with half a key set into it. On this night in St Austell, some of these morons were kicking people in the head and laughing about it with each other. It also had something to do with it being in some way permissible because it was a punk gig. They had most probably read it in their 'penny handout' or had it read to them by someone else, possibly their mothers or maybe a social worker that it was part of the punk thing to spit, punch and kick. It was great, like malcontent school children, 'Sir' was allowing them to express their creative talents.

I felt sorry for some members of the Fulham Crowd. They were very young and often got picked on yet they only wanted to travel to gigs and have a good time. I had had enough of one of these security types and, getting up from behind the drums, I hit him. It didn't really seem to have any effect. I turned around and got back behind my kit. We went into 'I'm On Heat' then, whack! I saw stars and found myself on the floor next to my drum stool. This symbol of atavism that I had just hit had walked by the side of the kit and nutted me in the side of my head. By now, the largest brawl I had ever witnessed inside a building was evolving. People were climbing on the stage, looking for a particular fight that took their fancy and then dived into it. I saw this chap, Dave, who had gone down there with Neil and a few other of the disco types from round our way. He got hit with a punch which levelled him and knocked him back a few yards, completely knocked out. I looked out across the dance floor. It was like an ocean of people fighting. I had a go at this bouncer type but he got me again. He knocked me down and gave me a few kicks. The aftermath was long with threats and concerns. Ambulances were called and some bloke who had something to with the place was threatening me, he was going to sue or something. I don't know.

Then I realised that the rest of the group had gone. I wasn't surprised. None of them were fighters, not that I was any good at it, just more stupid than the others were I suppose. I collected my bag from the dressing room, put on my trusted donkey jacket and walked outside the building with intentions of getting back to our digs. Then as I stood there I realised I wasn't sure where the place was. The rest of them had been given a lift, so I was told. After asking around I was given a lift to a road that I was told was close to the Guest House. I walked down a country a lane, not knowing where I was but following directions given to me by the person who dropped me off. I've always been afraid of the dark and never felt safe in quiet places, always more secure and less suspicious where there are lots of people, being anonymous maybe. Anyway, after battling with my neurotic childhood fears and not getting kidnapped by the bogeyman or raped by a gang of wayward schoolgirls who had given up their convent life to live in the wilds and search out portly punk rock drummers of a nervous disposition, I came to a couple of houses and thankfully the digs was one of them.

I tried the front door but it was locked and nobody answered when I knocked or rang the doorbell. There was the sound of music and of cheery but polite voices being raised so I figured it drowned out my knocking. I crouched down, opened the letterbox and spied through it. An elderly gentleman was passing so I called out to him. At first, he looked around a little confused as to where the voice was coming from. He opened the door but only slightly. Peering out, he asked what I wanted. I told him who I was and that I was staying there but he was having none of it, telling me that it was a private party, "A sixteen year old girl's birthday party, no interest to you, I'm sure." I tried to explain, going through my story again but he became a bit huff. He closed the door and walked off. I remained outside, looking through the letterbox. Occasionally a silver-haired woman in a gaudy party dress would pass through the hallway from what I took to be the kitchen into the living room carrying a tray or whatever, sometimes accompanied by an excited child jumping and bouncing at her side, most probably crawling for treats. I called out a few times but it was hopeless so I made my way round to the side of the house. A window with the curtain open was above a flower bed. I decided to go and knock on it or wave to someone. I trudged into the flower bed and found that it was full of bloody rose bushes. Looking through the window I saw the old bloke I spoke to at the front door and I spotted the owner and his wife who talked to us earlier in the day about this party taking place. There were elderly men dancing with children and a girl who was obviously the birthday girl was constantly smiling, wearing a party dress that seemed a bit innocent or young for a sixteen year old to wear. 'Maybe sixteen year olds have parties like this,' I thought; not that I would know. I had a closer look at her, thinking that maybe she was a bit simple or maybe I was just a nasty bastard and this was normal family fun and there, there by the little bar in the corner of the room was Pete, Nigel, Howard and a chap called Mark who followed the group about, all of them sipping at drinks and looking around the room.

The man who wouldn't let me in noticed me trying to catch someone's attention.

He stood there frowning at me. I pointed to Pete and the others at the little bar, pointing and giving him the thumbs up whilst mouthing, "there they are, I'm with them, ask him." The old chap tapped Pete on his shoulder, whispered something in his ear and pointed to me through the window. I continued to nod, giving the thumbs up. Pete looked at me with no change of expression, turned to the man and shook his head in denial before returning to his drink. The man looked quizzically at me. I mouthed "but I do know him." The man waved at me to go away and then got the attention of the lady of the house. Her face creased immediately into a mask of disgust. She came to the window regarding me distastefully. Putting her face close to the window she asked what I wanted. After telling her she told me that nobody knows me there and as I don't know anyone, I should leave before she phoned the police. Looking down to where I was standing, she told me that I was ruining her roses. I started to protest but she sniffed her dismissal and pulled the curtains together.

And there, staring at me, I saw my reflection in the darkened window pane. I jumped a little before realising it was me, 'Who the fuck is that ?' I thought. My face was lumpy and bloody, my eye was heavily swollen and blood from my nose had dried in smears across my face. I looked like a monster from the deep trying to gatecrash a genteel gathering. I started to back out of the flower bed but there were thorns everywhere. I eventually managed to disengage myself from her Ladyship's garden cruelty and returned to the front door. After much knocking, ringing and calling through the letterbox, the owner talked to me through the slit in the doorway. Finally, it all clicked with him. Letting me in, he mumbled how strange it was that my friends did not recognise me. "Yes," I said. I dumped my bag in my room, had a wash, change of T-shirt and joined my friends at the bar. Pete half looked at me from his glass and muttered, "Where have you been ?"

A week or so later we were to off on a long sea journey, it was further than the Isle of Arran; it was our tour of Ireland.
We parked our near clapped out old van on the ferry at Swansea and waited like condemned men, unknowing and not caring for the night's voyage to Cork in the Republic of Ireland. The management had told us a few weeks earlier that we had gigs booked in Cork, Dublin, Belfast and Port Rush. It caused a great concern to us, fear to be honest and I stood on that deck now that the time had come and pondered, "was this going to be the greatest of our 'miss bookings'?"

The Lurkers had no formal, established or recognisable political image. Our educational credentials spoke volumes on our formal grounding and insights, explaining in part our existence in a vacuum. There were the political groups around, loads of them but none during that era had gone over to Belfast. When groups did later on, it was amidst a marketing tidal wave, complete with art, dress, imagery, the posing, within a framework to exploit fully the situation but then, unfortunately, I found that is in the main what a lot of people respect or are conditioned to respond to. I remember thinking, 'why us ?' We, I, was naive in nearly all matters and pop politics were played out by others, why were we going there ? Let's admit it, we, I, was scared. Belfast, for me, conjured up images of news stories on the television late at night with buses burning as they lay on their side. Or bleak, boring looking estates where it's always pissing down with rain and close up camera shots of the tape used by the police to cordon off an incident with a couple of youngsters riding their push-bikes in the background. An image that stayed with me from Belfast was of a photograph I had seen of two young girls who had been tarred and feathered by the IRA for fraternising with British troops. The young girls were tied to a lamp post with their heads shaved, the black gunge and muck dripping from their heads and down their faces. But what struck me as poignant about this image was that they were wearing Bay City Roller outfits. There they were, in the boots, short trousers with big flares having a wide tartan trim sown onto the bottom, a Bay City Roller scarf tied around one wrist with their faces staring up as if trying to look away from their experience. At first I thought it was rough justice for dressing like a Bay City Roller fan until I read the article.

I later thought that I often notice the clothing a person wore in grim photographs of people being killed in incidents around the world, wondering if they ever thought that was going to be the last time that they were going to wear those shoes or what a terrible fashion to die in. And there, the innocence of being a young girl, joining in with normal contemporary fashion, dressed in clothing maybe their mothers had to alter and add to in order to have the 'Roller' look and now, tied against a pole. The face of Eric smiling emptily on the tattered end of a scarf. This was never in the minds of the marketing people who pushed the Roller image.

We started the tour with just enough money for one night's accommodation that was in some kind of dormitory *cum* flophouse place. I remember waking in the night with the police walking around the room, truncheons out looking for someone. Anyhow, Cork was like a set for a 1932 film. People waiting for the last dance around the walls of the hall. 'Aliens for aliens' I thought.

Dublin was a spectacular 'miss booking'. It was a dyke bar that didn't sell beer, only wine and did they whine. They employed off duty policemen as bouncers.

Howard kicked up and was upset at their heavy handed approach. He wasn't going to play because of the way they abused the few interested people who wanted to see us play. So they threatened him. 'Irish eyes are smiling,' yeah sure, the nasty miserable bastards. It must have been an arty, swanky place because Bob Geldolf turned up. I didn't speak to him but Howard did, telling me that he was an arrogant fucker, a university type who knew it all and according to Howard didn't drink. But, all this did not matter; our real concern was Belfast.

We left the motorway and entered the cramped Victorian streets of Belfast. A fine drizzle seemed to lay a seal over a place that harboured threatening intent. Shadowed by hills and the Black Mountain this forbidding place was different in all ways to what us boys from suburbia had known or experienced. Staring through the window of our van, we searched for street names that would take us to our hotel. There were signs reflecting a life and experience that told us this place is foreign. The murals, some garish, some of dark silhouetted gunmen, there were flags and messages, slogans and names of people having a striking significance to the inhabitants of this place, which spelt suffering. And, here they were, whatever or however the media presented and misrepresented the place. I looked at the people; small elderly women, bracing themselves from an hostile wind that blows wildly through the clothing and souls of those people going about their business in that town. There were different colours painted on kerbstones, words daubed like 'H-Block'; we didn't know what it meant, we shared the same media, the same government but this was a foreign land. We were lost, in all directions. An army vehicle pulled alongside us. Plug (Pete Edwards) asked one of the army blokes for directions. They all turned as one and looked at us. He came from Croydon if I remember correctly. He asked us what the fucking hell we were doing there. We told him that we were in a group. It was met with silence. A punk group. We gave our name. It meant nothing. The silence continued. One looked at the other, then one of them said, "you must be fucking mad". It was strange. The faces of the young soldiers, looking out of place. To me, most of them looking like Northerners. The UK's cultural exchange scheme was an edgy one, fraught with cynicism, dissimulation and apprehension.

We booked into our hotel and experienced a security that was from a life we just simply were not used to; then were too worried to venture around the area for a drink. Remember, at this time there was no debating on the television. Many people weren't allowed to be on the television. There was no positive promotion of Ireland in general, no winning football team, a film industry, romantic images of intellectually but tough young men in films and even adverts. It had not yet become cool. No, it was fucking cold, we were 'out in the dark'.

That night we played in a little place called The Pound by Queen Elizabeth Bridge. We were to play two nights. The place was packed and the reception was wild and friendly but I thought maybe too hysterical, like people starved or denied access to participate and belong with the flow of normality. This over exuberance carried the night on, with us knowing nothing of the troubles. People were asking what we thought. I tried to understand but mostly the answer from us was about the difference in beer.

An alley ran from the club to the street outside. I was standing outside by the opening to the alley talking to a bunch of young blokes before we went on. The talk was mainly about no one coming over to see them and they spoke of things I didn't know about and using words like internment. I did not even know what that meant. One of the lads kicked a can into the road. Just as this happened, they turned and ran back up the alley. I stood there looking about myself as a sort of Land Rover pulled up sharply and these police types jumped out carrying different looking guns and took positions of aiming rifles at roofs. I wasn't used to seeing guns banded about in the street. It shook me and I realised that I was in that distant land I had seen on the television. This copper barked at me, "What is it ?" A cold fear spread through me, I was numb and didn't have a clue what he was talking about. I think a simple smile formed across my lips. In his hammer drill tone, he rasped as he repeated his question, "What is it ?" He gave me a clue by nodding at the can lying in the road which seemed to me now to have taken on an extraordinary stillness as if this was significant in some way. I think my smile became more ridiculous as I offered, "A can, a beer can." His eyes had fixed themselves to a place about six streets behind my head. "Pick it up," was his order. I stepped into the road and picked up the bloody can. It seemed to take an eternity. I could hardly move. "Put it in the gutter," came the soothing lyrical voice from Bubbly Billy, the Bobby from Belfast. Mind, I was in no mood for micky taking at that moment. The yellow stripe running down my back was glowing to its own little inferno. He went on to ask me where I was from. I told him and what I was doing there, thinking he might be impressed, become a bit friendly or even apologise, but nothing. He gave a short nod to his colleagues. They jumped back in the fun wagon looking ahead grimly or at me and headed off, off to play at a children's party, a Bar Mitzvah, tell jokes at a funeral, I don't know. I can't remember if I waved goodbye to them but I turned, mechanically, walked up the alleyway and went back into the club.

The lads that I was standing with in the street were with the promoter watching what had happened on a security screen.

"Blimey, that was weird," I said. One of the lads said,

"Christ, I thought he was gonna shoot ya." I looked at him.
"That's what they do here you know," he said.

I found the rest of the group by the bar. I walked up to Pete and told him what had happened. He turned, looking from his drink to me without expression, "Mm, well, that's what you get for talking to people."

We went on to Port Rush for the last gig, a seaside place having echoes of Victorian Britain in its architecture and with armoured cars rumbling lazily along, absorbing the fragrances, colours and sounds that make up the peace and idleness of a carefree holiday afternoon. A young lad joined us at Belfast. He slept on Howard and Pete's floor in their room. He asked what living in London was like. He told me that his 'ma' had bought a television only it was wet when it was delivered to his house. In between his mum choosing the television in the shop and it being delivered, a bomb had gone off in the shop next door or nearby, damaging the shop so they had to put the stuff outside on the pavement and it was raining. He saw the irony of the situation and thought it funny. The next day we dropped him off in Belfast. I didn't know if he was a Protestant or Catholic, it didn't matter to me, we didn't know anything about it all. But, I had gained insights, the story of his mum and the television, the images and tone in the voices had raised emotions in me. Maybe we were approached by the politico's but it all went over our heads. Seeing the dumb expression on our faces and our talk of about having a drink, told them that we were not on board. Yet, in talking of beer and sharing sentiments to the ordinary small things that make up a person's life, I look back and see at least it was real. There was no posturing and leaflet giving or speech making about subjects that affect the lives of people and I came away from the place thoughtful and wanting to know more. I don't think it was shared with other members of the group but that was alright, they were not contrived, there was no hidden agenda, they were just making of things as they can in order to get by.

We were going up in the world. The management told us that we were to get a car to go around in, albeit an old one and a Tour Manager. His name was Jeff, coming from Lincoln with that dry whining accent that tails off at the end of a sentence, giving the talker a sound of being chronically bored with what they are saying. Complete with cowboy boots and an American tour jacket from some mid-west band, his hair was long and carefully coiffured. Jeff tweaked his shades and hit the road with The Lurkers. There was to be no beach parties. Having once drove some members of The Eagles from an airport to their hotel, this ride was going to be a bit more, well, earthy, violent, miserable and leading Jeff to the place where marginal man stands, far away from the sparkle of the stars.

Jeff was a first rate hypochondriac. He travelled with a veritable chemist shop, something for each ailment but, he was a good bloke and I liked him. He had a great driving style, never over sixty but we seemed to get where we were going quicker than hell driving, a real pro.

By this time, the punk thing was hitting mainstream attention, with caricatures of the fashion to be used in sketches of comedy shows on television too crap to mention. What for one young person was the embodiment of difference and being his or her symbol to retaliate against it all, had quickly been digested and ridiculed in a machine-like use to entertain people who watch and accept with their soporific gaze as the cathodic rays burn in another dose of bewilderment. The media often portrayed the punk as tough when, in the early days of the movement, it was inhabited by skinny art school types. The classic punk look of Mohican, leathers and bondage trousers became a uniform for some, interchangeable with their disco clothes. Certain areas of the fashion became more conventional, the neatly pressed jeans and The Jam printed on a clean, neatly pressed T-shirt was the riskiest many a young lad's nod went into the punk direction. But, there you are and the fashion swung into the arty, squat/ hippy types with a political awareness, this being the principal selling point for their band as they stood staring meaningfully at the camera, all in uniform and accordant to the cause. Usually fronted by the head boy, a little more equal than the others, often a fallen art student singing songs about living in a cardboard box and eating spit and shit for breakfast but always standing in front of his group. Their name would be something like Dick Shit and the Razors with Dick Shit having a separate recording contract, if it came along, from the Razors. Hailing from the wastelands of the midlands, although 'Dick' grew up in Weybridge Surrey, don't you know ? He later went on to compere his own television show, two of the Razors die and the other two become security guards or something like that; anyway.

At some gigs, the Dick Shit character would approach me, asking questions of our soundness. On finding out I was quite friendly and leaving myself open, he would accuse me of not being socially aware. His fingers would point, there was a purpose, being focused, telling me about the government, how people dress, how I should know about poverty. I would sometimes look at his uniform, the designer, grungy/squat/punk/hippy statement, and often, the next morning when sober, I would think, why didn't I punch that deceitful sod in the mouth?

No, we were not focused. For me, unconventionality in our society was experienced through the disparate people I met, who look like normal people, standing aside, often confused, sometimes threatening and feeling threatened. I would invariably end up talking to bouncers who were distracted. Starting their conversation within the accepted limits of a bouncer's world but then spin off into something like telling me that his wife had left him but it was alright because he knew where the bastard lives who went off with her. Then the bouncer's cousin would join in, saying things like he had just come out of hospital and that he collects ants and he keeps them under the eyelid of the family dog who is dead. The bouncer would nod to confirm this or that his cousin was mad. They would squeeze my arm and frantically seize my hand as if the information was forbidden and precious. The lone ranter; his mouth close to my ear, then standing back to check the response in my eyes, telling me that by "merely shaking your hand I can tell your ancestry, I've wanked so much wearing the same pants for years, never wash 'em, just think like, I'm not a Catholic but all those would be children, caught in the elastic of me underpants, all screaming bits of nearly children, that's what I call 'em; I hear 'em screaming as I walk down the fucking bastard road 'an there's me, looking around all embarrassed like 'cos of the noise of the nearly children stuck in me underpants." He would then step back, casting a querulous eye over me, "Hey you, you bucket of wasted cum, when you playing here next, eh ? You ugly fucker, nice to make your acquaintance." Anyway, something like that. I was living in a twilight world bristling with senses that told me that the country/society was an open asylum. I just happened to veer off from the polished corridors into the rooms of some of the patients.

'Touring'. Three boys and a man go on tour, all living at home except Howard. Pretty racy lot these Lurkers. Howard had the attention of girls. They said he looked like Paul McCartney. They liked his boyish looks, he was interestingly sullen and moody and he was always a miserable sod who drunk like fuck. Whatever time we got to bed, the next morning, as we travelled to another town, I would hear the tssht as a can of Newcastle Brown was being opened in the back of the car. There he would be, sitting there, looking out of the window as we approached the town, a sneer would form on the side of his colourless face.

££££££££$$$$$$$$$$$$$$$$££££££££££££££££$$$$$$$$$$$$$$

Whumpph! A twenty million dollar missile explodes into a twenty cent hand barrow: people clap and congratulate one another, it's a long way away from where they are, thank God for sanity. It is the revenge of the righteous on children who eat sheep shit, grass and water for breakfast.

$$$$$$$$$$££££££££££££££££££££££$$$$$$$$$$$$$$$$££££££££

Most of our gigs were not particularly memorable. Although I smiled at the antics of Adam Ant, we played with him again. I think it was down the Electric Ballroom. Adam was to support us and this did not go down very well with him. I assume he saw himself above it. He was a strict governor giving out orders to his Ants and it seemed woe betide any dissension in the ranks. His trendy bunch didn't like us, neither did a lot of the mainstream, student/ hippy types who were catching on to the new wave of music. The Lurks appealed to a selective band in what was already a minority area.

Every group has bad nights; indifference or 'miss bookings' are one thing but having boring fuckers taking the piss is another. Sitting there like something in a freak show as the weekend bikers or whatever do a conga dance around the place and do their mock USA 'wo wo wo' for more made me think that a law for possessing a personal hand gun might be a good thing. It was on one those types of evening that we played this pub in Wembley. After the gig, I got a lift home by Tim, an old friend of mine who I used to work with on the buildings. That evening the rain was extraordinary heavy and the radio played one Elvis Presley song after another. Tim pulled up his old Cortina Mk 3 outside my place and we had a chat about the amount of Elvis being played and if it was possible that the King had died. The DJ spoke in those sombre tones that they reserve for such occasions soon answered our question. I thought of Elvis Presley, of how he ended up, a slave to cabaret. I thought of the people doing the conga dance earlier on in the evening who really want cabaret. Those people most probably got what they wanted, years later in the Beaver Lounge at Butlins in Minehead or whatever, listening to the raunchy guitar licks of a Clapton impersonator, nodding their heads meaningfully whilst their children are doing a conga dance in the Junior Beaver fun lounge. And so it was, they carried the King's chronically bored bulk from his heartbreak hotel for the lonely, set in a desert, created from neon, concrete and dreams.

A year on from that night, the punk thing had taken off. Established show biz types grooved at the hip places where music of the in movement was being played. It must have been a mistake that Omar Sharif turned up at The 100 Club the night when we were playing there. I couldn't believe it when someone told me that he was up at the bar, he must have thought there was some kind of jazz band playing; still, hard luck. However, playing down The Nashville when part of the crowd had come down to exhibit their brand of challenging behaviour was more common to our experience of playing gigs.

One Saturday night, a bunch of blokes who had been to see Chelsea play, came down The Nashville. On arriving, they met blokes who had been on the drink, both having no interest in the music, just there to cause fights and ruin someone's night out. The fight erupted and it was a rough one. One bloke jumped on the stage and pulled a trowel out of his bag. I took it that he was a bricklayer by his clothes and not having gone home for a wash and change. He then jumped into the fight brandishing this trowel. There were people in the crowd who often came to see us, one of them being a chap called Jerry. Although I didn't know him then, he was pointing at us, staring, shouting over and over as the fighting went on around him, "We are God's lonely men."

It was more than unfortunate that many of our gigs had trouble and there were many that I didn't enjoy playing anyway but I always liked The Marquee; it was my favourite and it felt like playing there was the right thing to do. I used to go there with my brother when I was fifteen, along with Plug (Pete Edwards) and Howard Wall. I used to tag along with them, not so much enamoured with the music but always wanting to be a drummer. So it was, we regularly played down The Marquee, packing it out. It's a bit of a trait of mine but I didn't realise at the time what I was doing. Nevertheless, I must have enjoyed it but don't ask me what was happening for, most of the time, I was unaware. Being pissed all the time, I used to measure gigs by the amount that I drunk; it was an eight pint gig, a five pint gig or thirteen pint gig: art and beer.

Nigel's lot was not as he would have wanted, pulling the short straw he always shared a room with me; the tight rhythm section. The tall thin artistic ones, Pete and Howard, always shared together. I always felt that for Pete, the thought of him sharing a room with me was some kind of anathema. If I ever had the impudence to enter his room, he would point his thin crooked finger at me, "leave" would be his shaky behest. Which made it all the more funny when one night, the only one I think, Pete and I had to share this room but, better than that, there was just the one double bed. This we shared but Pete wouldn't get under the covers. Anyway, poor old Nigel used to get fed up with me or my neuroses at any rate. Too much alcohol didn't help. I was always sleepwalking, talking in my sleep, shouting, jumping up and accusing imaginary demons of persecution. I would often drink Benolin, a bottle or two on top of ten pints but still the demons would work and worm their way into 'My Heady'. On more than one occasion, Nigel would take his blanket and sleep in the bath. I sometimes woke to find that I had been shouting, with Nigel looking at me, saying, "you mad bastard, I've had enough." Once, I thought there was a mouse in my ear and someone had put it there. Anyway, Nigel went on about that people join a rock band for girls, parties and decadence, "and what do I get ? A fat weirdo with his vitamins, tablets, chest expanders and screaming nightmares of mice in his ear, just my fucking luck."

Maybe he had a point but I didn't do it on purpose and, worse for him, was that he couldn't escape, not being allowed in the hallowed ground of Pete's room. I reminded Nigel that it was better than getting a peck on the cheek from a paedo teacher on a school trip, so he should take it that things are looking up. Anyway, what did he expect, leaving mother to go on tour ? I would laugh to myself, the glamour of being on tour, on the road, romantic stuff, Jack Kerouac and Nigel Moore, although he did get his way with some desperate woman, once, maybe twice. The world of having droves of groupies was not in the world of The Lurkers. There weren't the hangers on from the aspiring arty brigade whether it be literary, music or from the clothing sector of fashion. We did not have the ex-teacher type wearing his or her 'out of work' freedom of expression clothing; we, it, did not fit. I often think that we didn't put up a barrier. In fact, it is the opposite and there is no barrier. It is that which makes it uncomfortable for others to engage. As there was no social or personality creations to be negotiated with, we were just being ourselves and it often offends if a person is just being themselves, it can make people feel insecure; in a way, exposing their own fears, seeing themselves as being false. How to win friends and influence people !

Yet, The Lurkers did have quite a big fan club. We saw it important to liaise, communicate and hopefully have a close relationship with those people who liked the group. As with all groups who have a bit of success, people write to you and want to know things about the group's activities. The Lurkers' identity lent itself to the singular person out there. Pete's songs of mad girls, boys who were on the outside and our attitude drew the attention of those people who felt they could relate. Good. One of the letters written to me was from a young man saying that his mum said that I could flip manhole covers like tiddlywinks. He finished his letter with the hope that we could meet one day so that we could have an arm wrestle; it would 'make my dream come true'. I think it was he who sent £5 for me to have a drink with my friends down the pub; we had good fans. A while later we played a small and crowded place in Nuneaton. Howard tapped me on my shoulder and said, "You have a friend." I looked around myself, then followed Howard's gaze. A small, very thin and pale young man with greasy hair was staring at me. He was very sweaty and nervous. He wore an unfashionable rain Mac, "He wants to give you an arm wrestle," Howard said, his face not changing expression then, sardonically, raising one eyebrow. I thought to myself, 'was this he ?' I turned slowly. Howard maintained his look, close to my face. We sat at a table, assumed the position and arm wrestled. His eyes didn't leave mine as he put no effort into the act. His hand was wet and soft. It was inane, maybe weird, he was pleased. No, 'Lurker' world was not for the main park players. As my friend Tim, the one who gave me a lift home the night Elvis Presley died, said to me after we went on Top of the Pops, "Are one of those trendy journalists from a magazine or paper going do one of those life style articles ? You know, living in the trendy flat in Chelsea or St John's Wood. At home with the celebrity; showing off the interesting interior decoration of the chic pad followed by a list of favourite restaurants, clubs and most interesting people ever met at a dinner party." Mm, anyway, it was a good gig and God bless the wrestler who brought his personal performance to Nuneaton that night.

The individuals we met and who approached us were like the group itself, taking residence alongside the action from those who do the pushing and shoving in order to mould the ground they will stand upon and own. I was realising that it was not just music itself that was the principal factor in contributing to the function of groups like The Lurkers. It was to share with others a feeling of difference, a flaw inside, a constant feeling of an impending doom, of not being *normal*, feeling crushed whilst watching others. As I understood it, Punk gave the outsider something that did not exist in the mainstream before. What it offered was as various as the people and their perceptions. There were many people out there. I was meeting those who felt this alienation. The structural protest, waving a banner for an issue or standing at the front of the crowd, this was not for them. No, it is not to belong; to feel that even one's physical presence is felt out of place and not to be part of the fickle dictate of fashion. The years of anguish, of feeling odd, outside, strange, different and then to connect, to feel a warmness, to smile and say 'yes !' It could well of been all wrong, misconceived, a misplaced emotion at just another fashion movement.

One night, Pete (Stride) and I were in The Nashville having a drink and watching a group when this chap who, to me, looked like a fifty five year old business man gone mad, tapped my shoulder and said 'hello'. I returned the gesture and watched this bloke walk off. He was staring at me all the while. Pete said to me, "That's made your evening, then ?" He told me that the staring man was Keith Moon. I looked over at him and he was still staring, so I went and spoke to him. He told me that a chap called Pete Butler pointed me out to him, he was a personal minder/chaperon for Keith Moon, who used my local pub, The Coach and Horses. His conversation was pretty superficial until I told him that my brother used to watch them rehearse at the Young Vic in Waterloo years before. His demeanour quietened, becoming serious he looked closely at me. He remembered that Tony and Roger, the roadies, had brought Dave along. I said that my brother had told him that he had a younger brother who wanted to be a drummer and that he gave my brother Dave a bunch of sticks but I only had one left and that was broken; I used them as a boy, drumming along to Happy Jack on a chair. He was interested and I was surprised, this celebrity had an image to live up to but I am sure that I saw the person beneath, a man who valued those things that make us human. Unfortunately, a couple of right wankers, student/hippie/punk types noticed him and barracked him for being rich. He gave one of them his jacket as a peace offering and the tosser took it but, before he left, he wanted to buy me a drink. I had a light and bitter; he had a treble brandy, it seemed fitting. He warned of not letting lead guitarists get their own way before rushing to the door and disappearing into the West London night time with its sounds of clustering traffic and a seemingly emptiness. A couple of months later he died. I read in the paper's report that a hospital worker said he couldn't believe it was the body of Keith Moon lying on the bed. He said it looked like the body of a sixty year old man.

Things for The Lurkers were moving along and we had a gig at The Lyceum. For the Lurks at that time, this was a big gig. It was packed. We were in the middle of touring around the country, usually in little places, pubs and whatever. So, this evening we were playing back in London, a big night, a lot of people there and then some fans of ours, The Kingston Crew, started moaning at me about the group selling out. Charming. There I was, skint, a chap from The Chords who was playing with us bought me a drink and the Beggar's Banquet elite with hangers on were in a box having champers. I thought, 'what the fuck is going on, I'm more or less apologising for playing there'. I don't know what it is, maybe it's a thing of control and people felt they didn't own the group any more. Whatever it was, control was not a thing Howard Wall thought about if his beer strayed from his fingertips.

The Lurks were not destined to be big, maybe because of the music but also we were not equipped to deal with all that's involved in being big. On this night, there had been a stage show planned, of modest means for a lot of groups but for us it seemed very professional. A big sound system was brought in along with on-stage roadies. There were these glittery things hanging down being caught in rising lights and swirling dry ice giving the effect of a moody mist. I looked at Howard, I thought to myself, mist rhymes with pissed and he was moody. We had our part to play in bringing together the choreographic effects. All that was asked of us was to start playing at a given signal. The curtains parted, the mist swirled, lights were set and the glitter glistened in expectation for our grand launching into the first number which would trigger some explosion or whatever. Anyway, we all piled in on cue, except Howard. "Stop, stop," he was saying, waving his arms to stop proceedings. "Stop, stop you cunts, where's my fucking beer?" He pointed to the side of the stage, "I left it there and some bastard's stolen it." I remember Pete gesturing for him to start singing but it was too late, the explosion happened, seemingly by mistake going off by itself and glitter stuff fell from above as dried ice rose from the floor and there was Howard, waving his arms about as he continued to curse and accuse people about the whereabouts of his drink. Someone at the front of crowd shouted for him to get on with it. This offended Howard further; he said. "It's alright for you cunts, you can go to the bar when you want for a drink but oh no, not me, I'm stuck here with this bunch of cunts with no fucking drink." And so it went; eventually a pint of bitter was handed to him, he quietened, turned round and giving the thumbs up to me he said, "Let's go." Being big wouldn't suit, I pondered to myself as we rattled through the set.

Also, the 'big lig' was not a feature of The Lurker's world; being invited backstage when The Ramones were playing at the Hammersmith Odeon was about the one and only. Jimmy Pursey was there. It was all talking bollocks and the Ramones themselves were in a world of their own. I tried to talk to Dee Dee about the Lyrics of The Ramones and the feeling of the writing but he was in American drug rocker mode, talking about a "a big sound system man." The chip shop around the corner from the Odeon was a familiar haunt of mine. I went there, taking solace from the chattering, vying and crawling of a sewer world rampant with spiky hair, wide eyes with looks that make you transparent if a more interesting prey is spotted and faces that contort every emotion to an accentuated extreme.

We met Mick Glossop again and recorded a single, Just Thirteen, in a studio down The Goldhawk Road. I felt that the group was beginning to learn how to play, not brilliantly but to a level where ordinary things were coming easier to do, like for me coming in on time. Mick remarked about the content of the song and gave concerns to its suitability for being played and its acceptance in mainstream world. He said it was a bit risky with words like, "just thirteen, it's hurting." "No," said Pete with no change of expression. The single was released and sold very well - for about a week, until Beggar's Banquet got a call and a smack on the wrist from a watchdog group. The record got pulled from the BBC playlist as paedo songs were not hip. But Pete's song wasn't paedo, it was of a lonely girl and not part of some preconceived package planning for negative publicity. It was just a naïve venting; it was honest with its intentions of looking at the emotions of a girl on the outside. This was not good for The Lurkers in any future record promotion.

It was not only the content of the songs that didn't bear well for the image of the group, the behaviour at our gigs was giving us a name of being trouble. We seemed to be targeted by certain types who came to our gigs and caused trouble. It wasn't clear why these people came to our gigs. We played love songs about fractured people and I didn't feel that this was a reason in causing a subliminal reaction to their own insecurities. No, it was bad luck. Around this time we played the Woolwich Tramshed and the BNP had organised a plan of bringing violence to the evening's proceedings. The gig was full of fans having a general interest but also, meeting in groups around the place, were blokes in armbands who did not intend to spread Christmas good will messages to all humankind. The atmosphere was shit. About three songs into the set and that was it, eight hundred people became two hundred who wanted to fight anybody who didn't. The police and ambulance crews turned up and there was no encore.

The continual violence and trouble was ruining the gigs and nearly finished us. With our brand of disjointed love songs and wanting all who came along to see us to enjoy themselves, was a far cry from the contrived building of a rowdy following, such as 'rallying the troops' Sham 69 style. The creation of the rowdy crowd with an overt political allegiance was a risky game for Jimmy Pursey. It backfired on him though. He suffered for it and was mentally very strained by it all; and all in the pursuit of power and attention or some kind of control in his life. It wasn't very responsible either, encouraging certain people to become excited who invariably took it out on people waiting for buses and trains on the way home at night.

For a while Howard lived across the road from some of the Sham group. The guitarist, Dave, lived around Howard and his girlfriend's place. Jimmy would come round and talk. He saw the news one evening covering the troubles in Ireland and wrote a song about Ulster but he didn't seem to know where the place was. The other people in the room apparently had to tell him where it was. Yet, the meaningful lyrics and politically aware intentions suited the demands of aspiring journalists to jump on the Irish troubles bandwagon, saying how insightful it was. I suppose it was a bit like the Pogues who I met a few years later, not an Irish accent in the fucking group, playing to the student mentality, fuck knows what private school Shane MacGowan went to; the same one as Joe Strummer I suppose.

Anyway, another character that used to stay round Howard's was Chris Henderson, who got to be known as 'Chubby Chris'. I knew him when he was a young punk with pink hair. He was a keen follower of the group and sometimes used to help out with getting the gear in and out of places. Chris became, how can I say, a bit of a heavy figure, involved in football politics and taking full part in skin gang warfare. However, I always liked Chris, he was always pleasant to me and sometimes he was a good lunatic, in a humorous way. One time Chris told me his theory on being healthy. It was a plan that stood in contention with the Californian, neurotic, aerobic, robotic tribe of body authoritarians. His theory was that one had to eat a proportion of one's body weight per day in order to remain in good health. He told me that on that particular day he had eaten six fried eggs and a loaf of bread but he wasn't sure what he was going to have for dinner. I haven't seen him for years; but best of luck, I think he needs it.

The Woolwich Tramshed experience was, I believe, too much or the last straw for Jeff, our tour manager. We got a new one. His name was Dave Kennedy, a man who told fantastic tales and drove like a fucking maniac. It was because of his driving style I became a nervous wreck whenever I went on the motorway. He used to drive one foot away from the bumper of the car or lorry in front. This was very unsettling. Being 'on tour' meant very little sleep and mixed with the disturbance that heavy boozing has to the mind. One morning, on a motorway somewhere up north, it was pissing down, the articulated lorry in front of us braked and we found ourselves for a couple of seconds under the tail of the mechanical devil. He wouldn't listen, he lived in his world, a world of drama and exaggeration; meeting us he had found a home.

Dave appeared to accept, in a rather philosophical manner, that The Lurkers weren't hip ravers and some of the idiosyncratic behaviour, albeit just little things, seemed to feed his own grand madness. I remember, not long after Dave joined us, we drew the attention of the police in Leeds or Manchester, anyway, a Northern town, for being parked with one wheel up on the kerb. This young copper was sarcastic as hell as he gestured for Dave to wind down the window. He went on, "What a bunch; bet yer like yer drugs lads ?" I was sitting in the back, in the middle, Nigel on one side of me and Pete by the window next to this copper. The young copper saw Pete through the back window. This caused him to smirk and go on that he bet Pete was on heroin. He said this because Pete was very thin and his long face with deep shadowy hollows in his features could make one surmise that he was on heavy drugs. Anyway, this silly fucker of a copper called his mate over to share his fun in baiting Pete. Now, Pete could let his face drop into a look of sheer terror and this he did whilst drawing slowly from the pocket on the front of his jacket a little paper man. The man was no longer than four inches, his arms and legs stretched outwards and a little face had been penned in. Still having the look of terror etched through his gaunt face, he held the little man above his pocket. "What the fuck's that ?" the goading copper said as he reeled backwards, taking his colleague with him. The copper brought his enquiries to an abrupt end. Pete put his man back in his pocket and nothing else was said. But I was wondering about the little man. I imagined Pete cutting him out and drawing the face, alone, in a room, in one of the rooms during the tour we were on or maybe it was from a previous tour or maybe the man had been around for a while. I asked Pete where the man came from. "Why ?" was the reply. I told him that I hadn't seen him around before. "Mm; haven't you ?" That was all I got. I saw Pete look down at his pocket. I knew I would not get any further.

Our first few gigs with Dave were down the South West of the country, Torquay and Plymouth, both 'miss bookings'. He was catching on to what was in store. We had a tour ahead of us. It was planned to be a long one and it was called 'The Killer tour'. We had T-shirts printed. It started with a return trip to Ireland.

We set sail from Swansea on the night crossing to Cork. This time we had a bit more money but not much and the company of Dave Kennedy made the whole thing seem like a sinister, cold war experience. Maybe it was but in the short time since we played there before, the place had opened up to outside influences. We played Dublin, it was shit and with warnings of the pseudo, studenty pose of a place it has now become; then on to Belfast with our expectations high because of the previous good experience we had. Well, it didn't take them long to get blasè. We played The Pound again and there was hardly any fucker there. Dave McCullough, a journalist from Sounds came over with Paul Slattery, a photographer. We weren't in favour with many journalists to put it mildly but there were the loyal few. Mick Wall was one and there was Gary Bushell but my memory isn't good enough to name the couple of others although I appreciated their support. Dave McCullough was from the North of Ireland or Northern Ireland and he was a fan of the group. I think it seemed sort of surreal to him, I mean him returning to what I think he considered a provinciality of thinking, the indifference towards us and the dull nothingness of it all. "Oh, we had The Clash playing at The Ulster Town Hall," or whatever the fuck its called, "so we did," said some smug fucker when I pointed out the difference in the amount of people who came to see us the last time we played there. So it was.

The hotel had a bar and a trad jazz band. The drummer wouldn't let me have a go on his kit but we had a drink and so to bed. However, our rest was disturbed by a ringing sound and a siren with a repeated spoken message to leave the room because there was a bomb scare. I was out of the bed and got dressed, telling Nigel to get up but he wouldn't. Refusing to move, he dismissed any notion of there being a bomb and went on about the London Blitz. I left the silly sod there and went out into the car park as instructed. There was Pete and Howard with a blanket over their heads, protecting their hairstyles I thought and somewhere, most probably on the hot line to MI5 or the CIA was Dave

Kennedy running about the place. There was no bomb, in the hotel at any rate, so we all trooped back in. I returned to my room, soaking wet, I stood looking down at Nigel, turning his head he said, "I told you so."

The next day I met up with Dave McCullough and Paul Slattery and we went on a trip to Ballymoney. The place was like a conservative middle England market town, quite twee, except for two blokes I spotted who were walking down the pavement towards us wearing balaclavas and carrying rifles. It was weird, nobody was taking any notice of them and I deduced that they weren't in fancy dress and collecting money to send a local child to America for some kind of surgery. I turned my body and focused on the contents of a shop, standing rigid, my gaze frozen. Through gritted teeth, I hissed at Dave, "What the fuck's going on ? Who are they ?" He replied in a relaxed jovial manner, "Don't worry, they're on our side." 'Our side ?' 'Our side ?' What the fucking hell did that mean ? My fixed pose and my taking an obsessive interest in the contents of the little shop did not flinch for a second as I watched in the window's reflection the two gun carrying street entertainers pass behind me and then, only then, did I start to breath more easily. A warm feeling surged through my body. I breathed deeply and then stepped back sharply. Paul and Dave were watching me and also what I was looking at. In the shop window were shelves of tiny brightly coloured patent leather shoes for little girls. "Alright Esso ?" Dave asked in a questioning manner. I don't think anyone noticed.

The next task was to play up north, Port Rush I think it was but we cancelled it as Howard felt too ill. I had lectured him on the danger of drinking like a maniac and eating food in such meagre amounts that it had the nutritional value of a crisp packet and like Pete (Stride) eating only when reminded, as long as it was only every other day and in Pete's case a mouse would shove it back to you if offered, thinking you were taking the piss. But, there you are, my advice was not heeded. Howard continued in his way and calling me a thick, fat bastard, claiming that he was really ill. Mind, he did look bad. Our morale was flagging so it didn't take much for us to call it a day and get the boat across the water to Stranraer in Scotland. On the evening we arrived, it was freezing cold. We found a cosy place to stay in the centre of town and I ventured out for a drink. Ominously, Howard did not want to come, saying he felt too ill. He said he would stay in the warm and have some brandy. The following day Howard seemed worse. A doctor was called and for Dave Kennedy, a man who could dress up the most trivial of tales into earth defying feats of imagination, the 'Killer Tour' was stretching his state of mind; that being said, he did his job well. Anyway, the doctor said it was serious, he didn't like the look of Howard and I think he asked if Pete was alright. The decision was to get an ambulance and have it done quickly as the doctor felt Howard's condition was worsening. He wasn't sure what it was but he didn't like it. The ambulance arrived with orders from the doctor to take Howard to a hospital that was about sixty miles away. Howard was beginning to slur his words. It wasn't drink and the doctor suspected meningitis or something bad. One of the ambulance men asked if I could give them a hand carrying Howard down the stairs as they were narrow and winding, making the job difficult. I took hold of one of the corners of the stretcher and slowly we backed down the stairs. Howard looked up at me, staring, his face sheet white. I knew he was pissed off with me. I attempted to make light of it with jokey quips but I knew Howard hadn't forgiven me for not agreeing with him earlier when he insisted that he was ill and I kept on about having something to eat. "You fat cunt, I told you, I told you I was ill but you wouldn't listen, would you ? Would you ?" I looked at the ambulance bloke next to me and offered a weak smile. He looked from me to Howard who continued to stare at me. We got out into the street, flecks of ice were beating down as shoppers, idlers and the generally bored went about the Saturday ritual that exists in towns up and down the country. A few stopped and watched as we carried Howard into the ambulance.

"He's bad," the ambulance man said to me as he nodded at Howard. I nodded, Howard mustered his little strength and hissed at me, "You; I told you, go on, go on, go and have a drink, you." The malice was meant, the ambulance men looked at me and I nodded pathetically. Tapping Howard's leg in a friendly gesture, I said, "Ah well, I suppose you'll see the wrestling this afternoon in hospital ?" We backed out of the ambulance. As the doors were being closed, I offered a wave. "Fuck off," came the last words. The ambulance men gave me a confirmative nod, I hoped not in agreement with Howard. They got in and began their drive to hospital.

I stood in that high street and reflected. I had known Howard for years, seeing him at school when I was eleven he was a friend of my brother but I was never that close to him. I would never have thought I would end up in a group with him, going on Top of the Pops and travelling around together and here, standing in this foreign high street, freezing cold, watching an ambulance slowly make its way through the traffic, carrying him to hospital. I thought for a while that he might die. Sometimes a feeling of comfort and warmness can arise in oneself when having nothing to do in a place not known and there being an uncertainty hanging over what happens next, a bit like a child at school if the lessons or whatever are disrupted. It was Saturday afternoon, the wrestling was on the television in the main lounge downstairs of our hotel, Howard was in hospital by now and Dave Kennedy rushed into the room with a fireman telling people to get out of the building as there was a fire. Sure enough, there was a little smoke coming through the door.

Now, I have a confession to make and the reader of this, if there is a reader, might think me a nasty bastard but this is it anyway. A couple of weeks earlier I had bought myself a Bullworker, it is an exercise appliance for lunatics, like most of these things are. It was bought in a vain hope of keeping fit or rather, trying to get fit or whatever. Anyway, it was upstairs in my bedroom. I ran upstairs to rescue it and ignoring Dave Kennedy telling me that there was a good chance we would be "fried". I ran as fast as I could down the landing and then stopped suddenly on seeing the door to Pete (Stride's) room slightly open. There was shouting from downstairs. I looked at Pete. All I could see was just his head on the pillow. He was asleep and his long, thin body did not make a shape in the blankets. I started to enter but then thought, 'fuck it, there didn't seem much time, I'll get me Bullworker'. Listen, it was new. Going into my room I looked around for things to take and after a quick look around my other stuff, I decided to take just the bloody Bullworker. I then rushed out of the room and down the landing, stopping momentarily outside Pete's room before carrying on down the stairs. Everybody went outside into the street. I stood there holding the stupid bloody thing. Dave Kennedy stood next to a fireman and I told them Pete was upstairs. Dave me asked why I didn't get him so I told them what happened. The fireman gave me a grim look but the fire turned out to be just a chair that was smouldering after someone had left a cigarette to burn down the side of it. We all went inside with some Scottish shoppers watching the activity and me feeling a berk holding the bloody Bullworker and feeling guilty as fuck about leaving Pete in his room asleep. Pete came downstairs and I confessed, telling him what had happened. He did not speak to me for about three days.

Evening came and we toured the town's pubs in search of what I do not know. On entering a pub, we were aware of our accent. There was the look from the locals and then the half turn as they looked away and so on to another lounge. We went and stood next to the fire, attempting to find some warmth in the hard Scottish town that was weathering another cold winter's night. We stumbled upon a bar that was very smart with brass and mirrors shining from diligent cleaning, a roaring fire and a friendly, if formal, young woman behind the bar. I told her what we were doing as if she was interested. When travelling around, I often thought people would be interested, sometimes they were but usually it was looks and comments like 'you're not from round these parts ?' The bar started to fill with blokes who had been to the football. The crowd that came in first had Celtic scarves. I spoke to one of them about Celtic. He tapped a large umbrella as he told me of his brother who lived near me back home. The bar was getting packed when another crowd entered. This lot was wearing Glasgow Ranger's scarves. The atmosphere changed and, after a while, the Celtic fan that I had been speaking to told me to mind myself as there was going to be a 'rammie'. 'Mm,' I thought to myself, a 'rammie'. What the fuck is that but it didn't take an active imagination to surmise that it would be a piece of human interaction that didn't involve acts of empathy and the bidding of good will to those who harbour different cultural choices. No, a dead stillness fell upon the bar and a physical division between the opposing groups. It was as if by design, a parting, exposing a freshly hovered, rich coloured carpet that I pondered at, trying to gain some comfort. As in all these scenarios, there is a lone shout or smash of glass instantaneously before the roar of battle begins. It was the most brutal and vicious fight that I had been caught up in. The absolute venom, hatred or whatever exerted by these people on each other was frightening. We jumped over and under the bar in search of an escape route. The bloke I had been talking to rammed the pointed end of his long umbrella into the face of another man, the sounds of smashing glass and shouting became as one. We made it to the front door and just as I opened it a massive policeman carrying a long night stick came wading through the doorway. "It's okay, I'm English," I said to him. "Well, fuck off then," came the reply, which I dutifully obliged by shinning it down the street with the other cowards that made up the punk rock group known as The Lurkers.

I went in there the following night, partly because I couldn't believe what had happened. The same young woman was behind the bar, the place was clean and shining as before, nothing broken, as if it was a film set. I said to her that it was a bad fight the previous night. "Ah, that's just them, it's a Saturday night rammie," she said, polishing the front of a hand pump. I stayed for one pint, watching the barmaid carefully and then made my exit.

The following day we caught the night train from Glasgow Central Station back home. Dave Kennedy had to stay up there and deal with the business of Howard. We hung around the station area, too cowardly to stray far, what with the accent and Pete's haircut and look. It was bloody freezing, a winter's night in Glasgow and there they were, straight-backs, wearing just a T-shirt with a packet of cigarettes stuffed up a short sleeve. It was about minus nineteen for Christ's sake. We stayed in the station bar having a drink and waiting for the train that left about midnight. A bunch of young blokes came in, all loud and mucking around, then they heard our accent. There were questions of what team do you support, being a Fulham fan came in handy, it was deemed neutral by most people. Then one of the gang recognised us as being The Lurkers. His name was Kenny Crawford and he had seen us play. In fact he was the chap who jumped on the stage at the Silver Thread Hotel in Paisley about a year before. It was him who was wearing a kilt and bashing his head against Art's bass guitar; small world. Well, we had a good night, Kenny was the only Celtic fan amongst his group of friends, the others all being Rangers fans. I told Kenny I had a soft spot for Celtic after watching them beat Inter Milan in 1967. I had come home from school and there was an important football game on the television. It was rare for football to be on at that time and me being a football fan, it was exciting. I watched the match, being taken by this team with numbers on their shorts. They went a goal down against the Italian team after about ten minutes and eventually won 2-1. It stuck with me because it was exciting. Kenny promised to send me down some Celtic stuff and make me a member of the club. We bid our farewells out of the window of the train as it clanked down the platform. It had been a good night's drink with our Scottish brethren, they ran down the platform by the side of the departing train, larking about. It did not take much to make us happy I suppose but there you are.

The heaters didn't work on that train. The alcohol wore off and it was a long journey home that marked the end of the 'Killer Tour'. We heard that Howard had meningitis and that he was in a bad way. A week later and true to his word, was the Celtic stuff Kenny had promised. There was a shirt, badges and a letter. I kept in touch, sending him back our stuff. And so it was, the year was sliding to a halt. Howard came out of hospital after four weeks, just before Christmas. He seemed different, slower. The doctors said it was most probably the spitting at gigs that caused it. When I look back, it seems that 1978 was the year for us. We were caught in the rush of a new development but I feel that we didn't, for whatever reasons, evolve, adapt, grow or what the fuck you are meant to do.

I kept a diary at that time. The only entry scrawled on the first seven pages of the year was 'Drink', 'Drink', 'Drink'. Howard joined us for rehearsals in January and we did the last of our John Peel sessions. It was the last as a four piece group. We later did some boring shit with John Plain from The Boys.

Anyway back to about February 1979. Beggar's Banquet, who at times beggared belief, drew on all their wisdom and decided that The Lurkers needed a more pop, mainstream sound. Somehow, God knows how or why, our management contacted a person called Phillip Jarrell to produce our next LP. Now, Phil had an interesting track record, as they say, musically speaking. He had penned the massive hit in the seventies, 'Torn Between Two Lovers'. This song alone had made Phil a millionaire. He was part of a writing team for Tamla Motown. Coming from the deep South of the U.S. of A., he had identified a recording studio in Northern Alabama where he wanted to take us for three weeks and had intentions of making hit singles. He came down to see us rehearse, standing there in his mid-western outfit complete with the faddy dress and gadgets of the time. I thought to myself, 'give the bloke a couple of days to think about it and he'll change his mind' but no, he felt that he had "work to do." Phil was with his German girlfriend. She was older than Phil and having aspirations of being an artist in her own right. She took photographs of things. The photographs were snaps. It all seemed very Californian what with the accompanying philosophy that held self-importance; know what I mean ? They came out with us a couple of times to see a group and have a drink. It seemed absurd, like some kind of joke but it went on and it dawned on me that it was for real. There was no connection between us. The group did not harbour any hidden ideas or interest in the rock 'n' roll image of Cuban heeled, flying jacketed guys jumping in the Limo with its Stateside values. They weren't bad people, it was just wrong. He couldn't drink, he moaned about drinking when we went out, telling me that my complexion was terrible and disgusting and went on about buying "vi-tamins" and getting in shape. He said that my drum kit was too small and to get a "rack of mother drums"; as I say, absurd. What was he expecting ? And what were the management expecting ? And as for us, I don't think we expected anything. But so it was, we got passports, Phil had arranged it all, flying from Gatwick to Atlanta then a flight to Huntsville and from there a drive to where the studio was in Mussel Shoals, Alabama. Off we went; one big happy family. I had not flown and, being a raving neurotic, I was panic stricken. The group was being led into the home territory of Phil and his girlfriend with her camera at the ready. My blistering fear on the plane made Nigel very unsettled. He had previously enjoyed flying but towards the end of the flight the camp steward invited me to help him serve willing passengers their drinks, an idea to keep me occupied and very good of him it was as well. We eventually got to the studio late at night. What with the travel, nerves and booze, the scene seemed surreal, the people in the studio appeared startled, finding our manner and language alien and so it continued.

We were put up in the house of the chap who owned the studio and also worked there as an engineer; his name was Steve. The place is called Sheffield; Athens is nearby, just down the road to Florence. I wanted to go to America, my favourite films were American, The Sweet Smell of Success, Taxi driver, Midnight Cowboy; John Steinbeck is one of my favourite writers and I'm a Raymond Chandler fan. There was something of an intellectual democracy about their storytelling and acting; dealing with emotions that are interpreted through a broader range of characters, unlike the British approach, which seems limited by crass class stereotypes and where talent is only afforded to those from specific backgrounds, occupations and accents. And here we were; but where ? It appeared to be the middle of nowhere; it was fucking boring.

The place was a dry county, meaning there were no bars and it was illegal to sell booze; the luck of The Lurkers. I felt that Phil Jarrell fitted the image of the American living out an obsessed existence. They have a culture of having to take about one hundred and eight tablets a day, go to counselling that has the latest fad techniques, have psychoanalysts prescribe a structure to live one's life by and even when asleep, wear daft contraptions to aid rest and all the other stuff that goes with it. In short, it wasn't us.

We had language difficulties but the cultural differences and attitude made me feel quite alienated. Although there was something interesting in the big coincidence involving the second engineer. His name was Howard, an ex-Vietnam veteran who knew one of our local pubs back home in Ickenham. Opposite to the pub, The Soldiers Return, is an American base. Howard visited there a few times when he was put on office duties after having a bad time in Vietnam. The engineer, Steve, had a girlfriend whose name was Kay Kay. It later became evident that 'Kay Kay' was from a Klu Klux Klan family and in fact the whole area was a K.K.K. stronghold. A few weeks before we arrived, there had been a big rally or whatever and the remains of the props were still in the field where they held it. There were three places to buy drink; the police, the church, the K.K.K. and all people in the different groups were incestuously entwined. We were stuck in Steve's house and at the mercy of Phil Jarrell as he had a car. None of us drove except Nigel and it didn't occur to us to get one but Nigel most probably wouldn't have liked the responsibility and we weren't aware of the concept of car hire. Come to think of it, there most probably wasn't a car hire place anyway.

Still, there we were, stuck, watching television. On one occasion the Governor of Alabama appeared on the screen one afternoon between the adverts. His square cropped head filling the screen with blue eyes drilling out at the languid recipients, he bleated a message, "Do you know where your children are this afternoon ? Make sure your children go to school; fight communism." It was surreal, funny but put an edge on things. The wrestling was the only thing of interest, this being years before it came across to the UK. It appealed to my imagination. I wanted to become a manager. I had the sick scenarios all worked out in my bored mind.

One night when we were having a boring evening staying in the house which was something that I hadn't done since I had flu when I was about twelve, staying in at night that is, the front door opened and into the living room of the house walked a group of blokes. We didn't know them but they knew we were staying there and using the studio. The studio was about eight miles away. It was one of a group of studios in a swampland cut off from everywhere. The Mussel Shoals Rhythm Section was famous, playing on known people's records like Rod Stewart, I think and Doctor Hook. The one we were using was new and getting off the ground. These blokes must have heard that we were staying there from someone locally. It was a small place, just a string of shops and a railway cargo depot that had about two trains a day although they were about two miles long when they did come. The place hadn't really moved along since the thirties although it had freshened up a bit in the fifties. There was no franchised, conglomerate companies pushing their services with blaring neon and advertising. This was before the massive explosion of the American enlightenment discharging into every artery and reaching the faintest vein. It was slow, slow and slow. It didn't take me long to remember not to ask someone if they had the time. I used to ask only because I was so bored and thought that at least it was contact with people but it would end up in some stumbling convoluted ramble of non-communication and miss-understanding, all said in a dreary 'Deputy Dawg' manner and tone. People didn't know where England was and it was dangerous to say that you came from there as they thought you meant up north in New England. This would make you a Yankee and in that place being a Yankee was the worse anyone could be. In the main, people were friendly and like many insular places you have to know the rules and stick by them. It was a shame. In a way I liked the dreariness but what with the alcohol licensing and being under the power of Phil Jarrell, it was resembling one of those long boring summer holidays from school as a child. It was a stifling tedium that plodded slowly along.

Anyhow, getting back to these blokes walking into our house. These blokes who came into the room thought they were being hard. They were threatening and they set out to intimidate. Luckily there wasn't a black person in the group. They just came swanning in, sat themselves down and helped themselves to our drink that we had bought from members of the K.K.K. The ringleader opened proceedings with his most friendly and intelligent line, "What's your nigger problem like ?"

We looked at him. I shrugged and said something like I'm not sure. Remember, we were stuck in this place and didn't know anyone. Steve, whose house it was, wasn't staying around, he let us have it for three weeks. Everybody has heard stories and seen films of these 'Deep South' types. For all we knew, they might have had weapons on them. "What do ya mean, boy ?" he said to me. I mumbled on about it being alright and he stopped me, glaring at me he said, "Do you know the only thing I owe a nigger, boy ?" I shook my head. "A four by two up the asshole." He nodded at this, not taking his eyes off me. His boyfriends were warming to the game. I had a look at them. It would have been stupid to do something and in the immediate cause none of the group could fight. I looked at the main bloke and thought, if this was back home I would smack the cheeky fucker in the mouth but there you are. I nodded and offered a dry grin. We all did. The main bloke was out to goad me, saying I was the wrong build to be in a band and telling us of his time in "Nam" and it's only right for a man to fight for his country but he's told what to do by Yankees and Arabs.

They relaxed after a while, saying things like, "Just welcoming you to the neighbourhood, boys, that's all." They let us know that they knew we were there in the house and that they knew all the boys in the area and that they might pay us another visit and have a drink. They left. They did not make a return visit although one afternoon Phil drove a couple of us to a large shopping mall. I think that he thought we would be impressed by shopping ? Anyway, I saw two of the blokes who came round the house. They were with their girlfriends or wives, most likely shopping for chain store shit and frozen yoghurt. I took a look at them, they smiled, they weren't so lairy now. I thought they looked like a couple of gimps, hiding behind the language they use; 'watch yourself now, we're the good 'ole boys, 'we are mean,' and all that bollocks. I would dearly have liked to have snouted the bearded tossers; that's life, as they say.

As I said it was boring and disappointing. There was a small shop at the end of our road that was run by an old couple. It sold groceries, cigarettes and bits and pieces. I would walk down the shop for something to do and have a chat to the lady. I don't think she had a clue where I came from. One afternoon whilst looking at the ingredients of American cakes and reading the nutritional information on the side of packets of cheese, a consumer pastime that hadn't been introduced back home at that time, a couple of locals walked in. One of them, a tall blond imbecilic bloke in faded overalls stood next to me and said, "What's your nigger problem like where you're from, boy ?" I thought, 'here we go again,' and him calling me boy when he was about my age. I looked outside and saw he had got out of a pick up truck and that there was a few more of his type in and on it. I just shrugged and tried to explain where I came from, all the while sizing this bloke up. He was tall and I was thinking of hitting him with a bottle of something. "You a yella belly ?" he said and again I shrugged, noticing that the old lady seemed a bit concerned. He went on, "Don't like damn Arabs; nope and don't like Yankees" and "Why 'aint you kicking Irish

I didn't take piano lessons for long.

'Snaps' from our Alabama experience.

Pete Stride.

That just about sums it up – give with one hand and take away with the other.

P. Haynes Esq.,   28th February, 1979
137 Glebe Avenue,
Ickenham,
Middlesex.

Royalties due to 31st December 1978   49.95

Less: Advance   100.00

Unrecouped Balance   £50.05

Pete and Howard looking like he's forgotten the words, again.

Arturo, me, Pete Stride and Howard.

On the Isle of Arran, just off the boat. Walt Davidson, Plug (Pete Edwards), Howard, Pete Stride and myself – don't ask.

Mick Stone at the back with a cigarette in his mouth – I'm making an impression on a Scottish lassie.

Remember, 'Ask to hear it in your record store'.

Fun days.

'Golden Gig Tour' ?

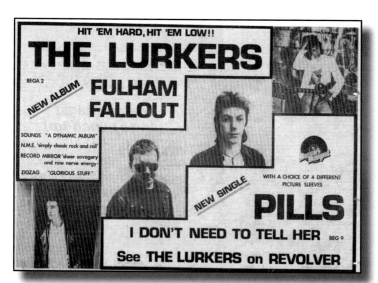

HIT 'EM HARD, HIT 'EM LOW!!

THE LURKERS

BEGA 2

NEW ALBUM FULHAM FALLOUT

SOUNDS "A DYNAMIC ALBUM"
N.M.E. 'simply classic rock and roll'
RECORD MIRROR 'sheer savagery and raw nerve energy'
ZIGZAG "GLORIOUS STUFF"

NEW SINGLE

WITH A CHOICE OF 4 DIFFERENT PICTURE SLEEVES

PILLS

I DON'T NEED TO TELL HER BEG 9

See THE LURKERS on REVOLVER

Collect all four sleeves.

THE LURKERS begin a British tour this week to coincide with the release of a new single 'Out In The Dark'. Dates are Peterborough Wirrina Stadium. (Friday), Wolverhampton Lafayette (Saturday) and Swansea Circles (Tuesday).

Pic by Mike Stone

We didn't spray our name on the wall – honest.

And it very nearly was a 'Killer' tour.

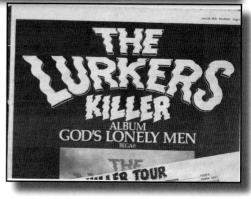

THE LURKERS KILLER
ALBUM
GOD'S LONELY MEN
BEGA8
THE
...LER TOUR

Me, Marc Fincham, Pete Stride — bloody freezing, with my personal sign behind us that we took everywhere.

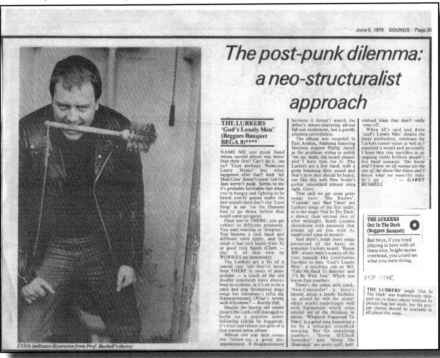

The post-punk dilemma: a neo-structuralist approach

THE LURKERS
'God's Lonely Men'
(Beggars Banquet
BEGA 8)**

NAME ME one punk band whose second album was better than their first? Can't do it, can ya? 'Cept perhaps 'Ramones Leave Home' but what happened after that? And 'All Mod Cons' doesn't count 'cos the Jam weren't punk. Seems to me it's probably inevitable that when you're hungry and fighting to be heard you're gonna make the best sounds (and don't cite 'Love Song' at me 'cos the Damned had to go down before that could come up again).

Once you're THERE, you get subject to different pressures. You start wanting to 'progress'. You become a rock band and different rules apply, and the result is bad rock bands (Gen X) or good rock bands (Clash — that ⅔ of that new ep WORRIES me immensely).

The Lurkers are a bit of a special case 'cos they've never been THERE in terms of press acclaim — a touch of the old double standards have always been in evidence, ie it's ok to be a yank and sing throwaway pop songs but Ickenham's intra dig (knowoterimeean) (What's wrong with Ickenham? — Rustlip Ed).

Despite the buying old media (snarei the Lurks still managed to build up a massive street following (cliché be buggered, it's true) and release one gem of a five-starred debut album.

Almost one year later comes the follow-up, a good disappointment. A disappointment

because it doesn't match the debut's senses-shattering all-out fall-out excitement, but a goodly selection nevertheless.

The album was recorded in East Avalon, Alabama featuring Motown singster Phillip Jarrell as the producer trying to polish 'em up, make the sound cleaner and I hate him for it. The Lurkers are a live band, with a great booming dirty sound and that's how they should be heard, not like this with Pete Stride's guitar smoothed almost outa sight. Grrr.

That said we get some great songs here: 'She Knows', 'Cyanide' and 'Bad Times' are Lurkers songs of the first order, as is the single 'Out In The Dark', a slower than normal slice of after midnight, South London showdown with paranoia that creeps up on you with its suppressed sense or menace.

And there's loads more songs possessed of the basic no nonsense Lurkers sound, 'Room 309', where there's a party all the time (sounds like Leverholme Gardens to me), 'God's Lonely Men', a touching ode to BO, 'Take Me Back To Babylon' and 'I'll Be With You'. Which just leaves four numbers.

There's the token slow track, 'Non-Contender' a loser's lament about a lonely bachelor 'so afraid he will die alone' which works surprisingly well with harmonies which even remind me of the Monkees in places. 'Whatever Happened To Mary' is a good song hampered a bit by a lethargic overthick opening. But the remaining numbers 'Seven O'Clock Somedays' and 'Sleep On Diamonds' are pretty naff, half-

realised ideas that don't really 'come off.

When all's said and done 'God's Lonely Men' despite the lousy production, continues the Lurkers tunnel vision as well as I expected it would and personally I hope they stay outsiders in an ongoing viable brilliant people's live band scenario: *'She know and I know we all wanna see the rest of the show/She know and I know what we want/So baby let's go . . .'* — GARRY BUSHELL

THE LURKERS
Out In The Dark   ○
(Beggars Banquet)

But boys, if you tried playing in here with all these nice, bright neons overhead, you could see what you were doing.

POP STAR

THE LURKERS' single 'Out In The Dark' was inadvertently shipped out to many places without its picture bag last week, but the proper sleeves should be available in all places this week.

ESSO: indicates dissension from Prof. Bushell's theory

Exactly!

The 'unspeakable,' well said Oscar

Myself, Trevor & Mark Wyeth.

ass ?" I must admit this one threw me a bit, this bloke knew something of geography. "Why 'aint yer fighting for your country, boy, you a damn Commie ?" It was an awkward minute or so before he finally nodded to his friend, they paid up and got in their pick up. I watched them drive off. The lady told me to be careful. She told me that not everyone is friendly, "and those boys are not." She told me that they knew where we were staying and that they would come round with "bats and things." 'Great,' I thought, this really wasn't Johnny Thunders meets The Ramones, crack the ice of decadence and enjoy the mess of the experience. No, this was housing estate ethics that I was accustomed to but it was a housing estate somewhere on the edge of Mars.

I was told later that Arabs were above Blacks in the hatred league due to the USA being held over a barrel on the price of oil in the early seventies. Yet Arabs were still way behind Yankees who were top of the list, seen as the cause of all wrongs. In fact, chiselled in the wall of one civic building were the words, "The South Will Rise Again." This wasn't graffiti, it was common authority policy and thinking; bad blood indeed.

On another occasion when I went down to the shop, I was talking to the lady and told her that I wanted to go to a bank. She told me it was a few miles away but her husband would give me lift. This excited me a bit, meeting people and doing something. I thought he might have one of the pick up trucks I had seen driving around, they are famous in films as the 'red neck' vehicle; maybe he would have an old classic as they were an old couple. She shouted to the back of the shop, telling the man to give me a lift. It was getting a bit embarrassing as I felt he didn't want to go out. She told me to go through to the back because the car was out there. I walked to the back yard of their home. It was traditional for that area, a fenced bit of land with chickens and miscellaneous objects scattered around, mostly scrap. I met the man and we shook hands. As I looked around for the car, he said to me that having business with the bank sounded "mighty bad". I told him that I wanted to cash some travellers cheques. What with the language and cultural difference, it sounded crazy to him and it most probably was. I continued to look around for his car, this being my only trip with anyone besides being driven to the studio by Phil Jarrell. The old fella walked to the side of the fence and there I saw a car that I hadn't seen at home for a while. It was a battered old three wheeler, having old batteries and a box of nails on the floor where the passenger seat would normally be. He told me that the seat had been removed for storage reasons. My first thought was that maybe he doesn't want to give his wife a lift anywhere and by the way she moaned at him to give me a lift, this was most probably the reason why. "Help us move the batteries and nails, young fella and I'll put a nice piece of wood on the floor for yer".

We drove down the road. I couldn't see out the window as my eyes were level with the door handle on one side and the gear stick on the other. He talked continuously. I couldn't hear him as I shook on the floor of the car. The sight-seeing tour was limited. I went to the bank, he got his bits and we drove back to his place. I got out of the car and walked up the road to our house, thinking about my afternoon. It was better than digging holes in the road with lunatics for a living but there was something missing.

The only other ride in a car I had, besides with Phil, was with Howard and a girl we met in the little high street. A young woman approached us one afternoon as we wandered around, asking us where we were from. I think she liked the look of Howard but anyway, we told her that the dry county thing was a bit of a bastard, not being able to get a drink and all that. She said that she knew of places where drink is sold and if we wanted she would drive us there. Well, in 'Lurker's World' this was seen as a major adventure. We jumped in and off we went. We were soon driving across fields by the side of woods, essentially way off the beaten track. The girl turned to me and I don't know if it was just me but I felt it came over a little sinister when she told us, "You boys 'ought to be careful." She went on about it not being safe getting lifts off people you don't know but it was alright with her. I glanced at Howard, he shrugged. I wasn't sure what to expect, her mad half brother with a chainsaw seemed vivid in my mind. We got to the place which was a caravan. She told us the name of the bloke that lived there and that he was a prominent Klan member. The girl knocked on the door of the caravan. It was opened by a massive big fat bloke with a beard, dressed in the uniform of faded denim overalls. We were invited in. The girl explained who we were and that we wanted to buy some drink. He spoke in that slow drawl, telling us that the "boys" would see us alright, showing us crates and bottles and more in an outside fridge. After buying vodka and beer, we got a lift back in the girl's car. She told us that he liked us and she started asking us about where we came from. She said, "What's yer nigger problem like ?"

The Northern Alabama's version of Intourist dropped us back in the quiet high street. Waving as she went, she said that maybe we could meet again and "party". That awful American term, "party" that has now spread through the British vernacular. Party ? With these people ? I wondered what their door policy on entry to the *party* would be. Nothing like having a nice relaxing time and breaking down barriers to meet new people and embrace different ideas but then again, there were plenty of these party people back home.

Most of the time I spent waiting. Phil got on my nerves so I would often keep away, sometimes attempting to go for a walk. There wasn't anywhere to really walk, just long stretches of road with fields where cotton was grown either side. I was learning about the American mind and its non-acceptance of individual thought and activity. A police car stopped me one evening as I was walking along and asked what I was doing. "Going for a walk," I said. They were not happy with this as if not accustomed to such liberty taking behaviour. The word and meaning of 'walk' was chewed over for a while. After questions of who I was and what I was doing there, their decision was to tell me that it was best if I went back to the house because it wasn't safe to just walk around and the concept seemed strange to them.

A lot of the time spent in the studio was often fraught with neurosis or plain boring. What the fuck were we doing ? Even the language began to grate, "Say what ?" Phil used to say when we tried to explain about the music lacking punch or just trying to convey general feelings. Phil used to drive to the house in the morning and ask each of us if we wanted to work that day. "Okay, let's work," he would say. After a week it was rare if all the group was in the studio at the same time. I remember Howard used to get annoyed with the language, saying "I'll bloody punch someone if they say that again." There was no hatred or dislike of Phil. Not at all, in fact I liked him but it was just a mistake us being there, that's all folks. Phil's girlfriend would call me over and show me a photograph of a fence or someone's head in the top corner of the frame. There is a limit to the amount of polite nodding a person can do especially as there were no bars to escape to. I hadn't mixed with the privileged wealthy who see themselves as hard working and having opportunities to present their work in the various forms of the arts. What I'm saying isn't absolute but its general. Seeing themselves as more insightful than ordinary people, harbouring elitist ideas about themselves and their greater sensitivity, getting exhausted if running out of some herbal supplement and finding out that the store hasn't got the jeans one wanted. I mean and all this in one day ? One needs a little pampering - "I know honey, it's tough." This was my introduction to the idle rich. Being poor and idle seemed okay but to think you had a talent like some of these people; you know what I mean ? Give me a break.

After two weeks I was going stir crazy. The dry county thing was too much. We hadn't been to a bar the whole time that we were there, in fact we hadn't been anywhere. It was twenty two miles to the Tennessee border. I was told that just over the border was a bar. This stayed with me, mostly all day, every day. After keeping on about going there and asking Phil to take us as there was no public transport and we didn't think of getting a taxi although I doubt very much if there was one, I ended up having a go at Phil to take us to the bloody bar. So, under duress, Phil drove us to this bar that was just yards or metres over the border, standing by itself on the side of the road. We pulled up in the car park and looked at the bar. Throughout the journey and the days before, Phil had gone on about the dangers of being a stranger and going into red neck bars. Phil told us that he would wait in the car as it wasn't safe, telling us they would dislike him and resent him, seeing him as sophisticated because they were land labourer types. This was interesting to me, all this shit we used to hear about there being no class structure in the USA. We left Phil in the car and went into the bar. There was a slight hesitancy on entering and I was being pushed forward to go in first but Howard brushed past me; he just wanted a drink. It was traditional American Bar world, spit and sawdust, pool tables and a jukebox playing country. The place quietened as one when we walked in, heads turned with no intention of diplomacy. I strode to the bar. "Where did he land from ?" was a comment I heard directed at Pete; his spiky haircut, solemn demeanour and long thin frame were of interest to the locals. It was nearly all men in denim bib and braces with a white T-shirt under checked shirts. The couple of women who were in there had the blond frizzy hair, tight jeans and cowboy boots sort of thing.

My eyes did not stray from the bar as I walked up to it. On reaching the bar I looked at this very tall bloke. He was blond with a long crooked jaw that turned his chin off at an angle. "Beer, please," I said but there was no answer. He stood there examining us and then checking around the bar before finally saying in a slow drawl, "Where you boys come from ?" "England, Britain, er, Europe, near Germany," I spluttered. He continued to look. "Sounds like a Yankee," came a voice from behind me. I turned, looking from the voice to the barman, explaining what we were doing and making it clear where we were from and where we were not from. A group settled around us but they were friendly. "Got Schlitz," the barman said, his eyes not straying from mine. We all agreed that would be fine. He returned from a back room and placed a crate of Schlitz on the bar. I went to put my hand in my pocket but he stopped me, "Hell, you boys 'aint paying for that, you've come a damn long way." He pushed the flat of his hand at me in a gesture that said the drink was on the house. We each took a can. The group that gathered around us was curious. Someone was convinced that Howard was in The Beatles and that we came from "Beatle Land". Howard became even more curious to them when bringing out a packet of ten Embassy Regal cigarettes. Some of them wanted to look at the packet. Howard gave them to a chap who studied it carefully. Aliens, we all were and I felt that if something grim happened there would no knowledge known of it except there was Phil waiting in the car park but he might of thought that he imagined the whole thing. And come to think of it, when we were in the bar, I thought that maybe I had imagined the whole thing. Insular doesn't fully explain the experience of the people who we were meeting but things got underway when the barman spotted that we drank quickly, offering me to take part in a drinking competition. By now we were buying our drinks but, for the purposes of our little competition, a crate was provided free of charge. The barman then came from the back of the bar carrying a bottle of moonshine. It was a dry potent clear liquid made from potatoes. We later had an arm wrestle on a specially designed arm wrestling table. I lost easily. The bloke was about eight feet four inches tall.

The locals were amazed at the drinking capacity of the strangers, who were speaking in strange voices and coming from a place that might have been a different land over the sea. Someone asked how we got to the bar. We told him and he checked through the window and there was Phil sitting in the car. A chap told us that they didn't get visiting musicians and in fact the bar had rules of its own. The question of race relations came up and we were told that a black man had been killed nearby and left by the trash cans at the back of the car park. He was there two weeks before they picked him up. The proceedings were brought to a close surprisingly early, about eleven thirty if I remember. As we left, the cold gassy beer I forced down earlier in games of "shot gunning" made a return, like a fountain it rained out and witnessed by the barman, who cheered as he stood outside the doorway of the bar. We left saying we would be back. A few people came out and gave us a wave as we got in the car and pulled away. Phil was keen to know how it went.

A few days later we made a return trip, only this time Phil and his girlfriend wanted to come in the bar with us. I explained the rules, meaning things not to do, like observing the patrons in the bar as if they were exhibits in a cage but Phil's girlfriend turned up with her camera. She was told that the camera wasn't allowed. People say 'you should never go back'. Well it wasn't a disaster but the evening didn't have the same feel about it. Phil and his girlfriend stayed in a corner and pretty much didn't speak to anyone. Some of the blokes told me they didn't like them. They were suspicious of those having quick talking liberal voices and advantages of education and rightly so, I had read my John Steinbeck.

The three weeks were up and the LP was sounding like shit and that was it for our jaunt into 'rack n' roll'. We shook hands with Steve and Phil at the airport. It felt cranky and to put it mildly we were out of place. We all stood there looking at one another, nodding, giving the last pat on the shoulder, hardly anything being said, the farewell, God's lonely men. Before boarding the plane, I was stopped by the bloke at the checkout or whatever it's called, who went through my hand luggage. The case itself must have looked a bit odd as it belonged to my sister, Pat, who had used it in the late nineteen sixties. It was a small groovy, effeminate but functional piece for the young girl in a modern world. I hadn't really thought about it until watching Mr Crew-Cut give it a long look. He went through the contents, methodically but not with a neutral mind. All it contained was a set of chest expanders, vitamin and protein tablets, a wrestling magazine and a detective magazine having a feature titled, 'God told me to do it,' blazing on its cheap paper. "You've been keeping yourself busy whilst you've been over here; none of the girls are safe," he sneered. I grinned nervously, wearing a shiny brown suit and a blue checked Trilby hat that I had bought in a Salvation Army type of shop a few days earlier.

Back to Blighty and the promotional push was underway with photographs being taken for the cover of the LP. The management insisted on a bloke to do the photos who was arty and who came along with his girlfriend and a piece of red cloth which I presume was used as some kind of symbolism. The photos were taken on Wandsworth roundabout on a miserable day. We were all knackered and not enthused by it all. There were some young mouthy kids using milk crates as improvised early versions of skateboards. They clattered around the concrete humps and mini-pyramids as this bloke got his girlfriend to place this bit of red cloth about the place. It was nonsense.

About this time we did a few gigs in Germany. God knows how we ended up playing in a couple of them. One in particular seemed to me like a work's do, very clean people waiting to dance in a disco area with tinsel and mirrors. Maybe I was drunk. I took a walk around East Berlin. The Wall hadn't come down then. My dad was there in the war. A woman sniper had shot through the underneath of his lorry causing him to crash and injure himself. She had been hiding in the sewer. My dad liked the Germans and always told me of the stupidity of war with ordinary people turned into killers for the benefit of cruel useless fuckers. We drove through East Germany on our way back from Berlin. The Cold War was going strong with all the paranoia, suspicion and ignorance. Stopping at a village which we shouldn't have as we had strayed a bit off the official route, we found people regarding our car with interest. Some of the kids were clambering around it and pointing even though it was an old clapped out Volvo. Looking into the shops with their austerity and colourless presentations was weird because it was different. The fashion or style of clothing in the tiny shops made me think that maybe I had slipped into an episode of The Prisoner or the Twilight Zone. Still, they're most probably in fashion nowadays in some arty circles, worn by the children of Western millionaires with their concentration camp figures and pallid complexions.

On re-entering the West side of Germany, we passed through a sentry post that was a hut in the middle of drab fields. It was cold quiet and still. The chap came out of his hut wearing a furry hat and a small machine gun slung over his shoulder asking what we had been up to. Starved of people to talk to, we had a laugh with this chap, giving him T-shirts, posters, records and stuff. He said, "Ah, you beat group, like Beatles, Elton John ?" We drove off. The image stuck with me and slowly he became smaller, smiling, in one hand holding up the records and in the other holding his gun. The bleak greyness of it all. Where did he live and who would he play the records to ? I waved until he was no more than a speck and still I could make out a raised limb. Was he missing out on anything ? I wasn't sure but it made me sad and stayed in my thoughts as we drew into the suburbs of a city that became louder and harsher the nearer we got to the eye of a consuming chaos that is the magnet of our great experiment.

It was May 1979 and the UK changes. The Conservative Party are voted in with an overwhelming support for an ideological shift to what I am sure for many of those that voted for it are unsure. In a couple of years, alternative stand up comedians will look like bank managers, speaking in liberal prose but grasping for the ugly stage they lied about despising and eventually doing adverts for banking companies that fuel the plight of those that cause the entertainers to wear red noses, search their souls and preach from an altar for the poor to give money to a charity. And so the progressives returned to notions of pity not politics whilst creating a profitable industry around it. Other ideas and ideals from a fictitious past, sought to support notions of returning to decency, even though the society was also seen as a thing not in fashion. It was up to the self to interface and do a deal. The bristling, oscillating, self-creating individual atom was a heady sales pitch and bought by many.

A couple of years later, my Dad and me were watching Norman Tebbit on tele. Dad told me that he and many like him had to go to war because of people like Tebbit and his leaders. " He's using the language," Dad said. However, in 'Lurker world', life continued for the merry minstrels as they brought their song of joy to the expanded settlements of this great land and it's cheery inmates. We played a sports hall in Peterborough, a bland town with a bland place for us to play in. Yet, we didn't finish playing the planned set because a transit van was backed through the double doors and a bunch of blokes wielding baseball bats and worse came tumbling out of the van attacking anything that had legs.

The tour continued with us playing in Edinburgh. Howard and I did this lunchtime radio show that chatted about what was on in the local area that weekend. As we were talking to the bloke presenting the show, he announced that The Police were also in town and that they too were coming into the studio that lunchtime to have a chat. I slumped in my chair on hearing this and set myself for being fucking embarrassed. I hadn't seen or spoken to Stuart Copeland since I gave him the benefit of my great wisdom, my astute perceptive ability of prediction. No, since telling him that his group will get nowhere with a name like The Police. They had released a couple of the biggest selling singles for years, become household names, fantasy figures for schoolgirls and nearly every female in the land and beyond and I should imagine for a few men. We were playing at The Top Rank, or something and The Police were playing a place that was Edinburgh's version of Shea Stadium and their show was most probably being beamed to the seven nearest planets. Our chat finished and I thought we might be able to go before they arrived but it was too late. They came walking into the room and on seeing me Stuart Copeland smiled wryly and dropped arrogantly into an armchair. I had a fixed grin throughout. "Ah, thanks for your tip Esso. Since I took your advice, it's all gone down hill." I nodded in agreement at my stupidity. I looked at them. They all looked so tall as if fame had made them grow a couple of feet. The space in the room was swallowed by their charisma and booming egotism. Howard checked his watch and confirmed it was time for a pint. We left, me making a further berk of myself by attempting a quip at Stuart Copeland about if he feels that he needs to talk to anyone about his career, feel free to give me a ring and I'll see if I can get one of my staff to deal with it for him. We left.

On my birthday, a few days later, we were playing in High Wycombe and there wasn't much birthday cheer about the gig. It got nasty as a group at the front were there to take the piss. After being goaded and gobbed at once too often, Nigel took off his bass guitar and used it as a double handed club. I joined in with a cymbal stand but someone caught the end of the stand and dragged me off the stage. I landed on my jacksie and took a few punches and kicks whilst I was on the floor. The gig finished early and I took my birthday present of a swollen lip, eye and nose home with me.

The following night we were playing in Derby. It was an Indian cinema that did punk gigs once a week. The place was an old fleapit. It seemed weird having the gaudy coloured posters advertising forthcoming productions. At that time, the Asian Community occupied more of a marginal place in this country's society and for us to be down to play an Indian cinema made us think that this was a classic 'miss booking'. But, not so. The chap that let us in was the owner. He asked what happened to me, noticing the bruising on my face, so I told him my tale of woe and I was feeling pretty brassed off about it all. He sidled next to me and asked if I liked Indian food. I told him that yes I did and very much so. He had given me a bit of a long look when we met, I suppose having a crop, wearing jungle greens and boots gave the image that I might not be too friendly to him but that had now passed. On hearing of my miserable birthday, this chap wanted to give me a bit of a party. He told me that his brother would be coming down to the cinema soon and would I like to meet him. 'Sure,' I thought, it sounded alright to me.

We played the gig. I think it was a good one and, whilst the gear was being packed away, the owner introduced me to his brother. His brother had a thin moustache and a slimy smile. He wore an imitation silk shirt that was bright pink and such a tight fit the buttons were ready to ping from the material. His suit jacket and shirt had the same extra long pointed ends to the collars and lapels. This bloke could have got a part as a slapstick pimp character in one of the Bollywood films and I liked him. He told me that his brother had said about my grim birthday the previous night. Pushing his face next to mine and widening his grin he asked me through the corner of his mouth if I liked "the blue movies; with the ladies ?" I told him that I didn't mind. His eyes lit up. "I show you, you watch the ladies jig a jig." We all followed him upstairs to a room. I think that it was his wife who was standing behind a table who had prepared loads of Indian food. She was being helped by another woman, both in Sahrees and very nice and polite. An eight millimetre movie projector was projecting moving images of an Indian blue movie onto a white bed sheet that was pinned to the wall, this being before the time of everyone having a video. The characters on the film spoke in one dialect and another dialect was in subtitles, both Asian. The brother told me his wife had prepared the food. He went on to tell me that he was a bus driver in Derby but what with his brother owning the cinema, it was like show business, so he liked to contribute in "entertaining artists, like yourselves". He grinned his smarmy grin but he had no ill intent. I know it wasn't outrageous but it just struck me as mad. I would say, for me, it was one of the best nights that I had playing in the group. I didn't get drunk, it was just good to be with nice people.

At the end of June, we had a tour lined up playing the North East area of America. I was looking forward to New York, seeing the places Lou Reed, The New York Dolls and Iggy Pop had played. It was the home of The Ramones, Midnight Cowboy and Taxi Driver. The management had organised the tour with the promoter who would meet us over there. The promoter was Ian Copeland, the brother of Stuart; I felt that was a certain irony. Still, after a battle with neurosis of flying we got there ready to rock. We met Ian Copeland. He had organised the gigs and a van that was pretty well clapped out. I shook hands with him and he said, "You guys know my brother, he told me that he met you guys." "Yes," I said. He went on, "Well, my brother's band, they've pretty well cracked it, I guess." "Yes," I said. The thing that was dawning on my thick mind was that these Copeland's were high achievers. Ian was some kind of war hero, another brother Miles, was a big noise in music back in London whom Pete Stride and myself met when we were starting, the father held a top job for the CIA and I believe the mother was an eminent archaeologist. I don't know if there are any more of them but, if there are, they most probably own a country or have franchising rights to sell the Earth to some alien, if or when they turn up. They are people of purpose, from privilege, a position giving opportunities and confidence, professional people, not likely to shy away from some local authority person in a suit making demands for rent or whatever. I was not jealous, just interested.

Ian told us that his brother's group had used the van before so it might bring us luck. He was a good bloke. First up was Philadelphia and the conversations I had with the people whom I spoke to on those first couple of days set the scene for the rest of the outing in Uncle Sam's experiment. The place we were playing wasn't that great and I found myself outside the club talking to a friend of the bouncer. I'd had a few drinks and was going on that Joe Frazier was one of my favourite characters and that I knew this was the town that he trained in. The chap I was speaking to told me that the very gym that Joe trained in was just around the corner and that he trained there himself. He said that he would show me the place if I wanted. I felt it to be a kind of pilgrimage to see this place and others where great characters, for me anyway, had made something of their lives. We walked the couple of blocks to the gym. I patted the wall of the building and tried to look through the window but of course it was dark what with it being closed. I forget how the gig went but I was struck down by the most violent of stomach pains and vomiting which lasted all night. By the time we got back to New York the following day, I was coughing up hot blood. I stayed in bed and eventually the selfish bastards with me got a doctor to the hotel. Nigel was worried about sharing a room with me in case he caught some killer illness but the doctor put him at ease announcing that I had contacted an 'Argentinian' virus. I had a temperature of 105. The doctor said that if I was in England he would have sent me to hospital but, with no insurance, it would cost a fortune over there. He gave me a prescription for some tablets and told me to rest. That meant we had to cancel the gig we were playing that night in New York. But that was not in the front of my mind; dying in fucking New York was. The doctor made some typically New York Jewish aside remarks about the view from the window which was three feet before being blocked by another wall. He then left and I lay there seriously thinking this could be it. "Drink plenty," the doctor had said. This confused Pete as he took it that I should go out to a bar but I wasn't well enough.

Well, who likes being ill ? I know there are some people who derive something from it but I felt terrible and it tainted the rest of my visit. A gay porter used to visit my room and get drinks for me. I remember that he insisted that grape juice would be the best although it was just a carbonated canned drink like any flavoured cola type of thing. The following day I went for a cup of coffee in a café with him, feeling like shit. Catching my white sweaty complexion in a mirror, I thought, 'look at me,' sitting there with this chap. I knew he was well meaning, well I hoped that he was but, all the same again, it wasn't what I expected. The porter was a big fan of the theatre, telling me how he liked the English accent and that, if I lost a little weight in my face, I would look like Albert Finney. He thought that he was a brilliant actor. The conversation went on about cafes in England not having a rest-room and of how he thought it so disgusting, what with our rich history and Royal family and all.

We played the next night. I felt bad. It was like a dream, ending up speaking to a seven foot psychotic black guy who was the bouncer. He told me about astrology and how it's all worked out. The other bastards I was over there with continued to booze and talk, way after we had played the two sets which is standard practice in the States. I must say that in nearly all the places we played there wasn't a good crowd, sometimes it was very sparse. Still, the show goes on.

It's a couple of hundred miles north to the town of Boston from New York City and, with the van packed, it was wagons roll. We were playing in this tiny bar with a stage that was wedged against a window that looked out onto the pavement or 'sidewalk' outside. With my position at the rear of the stage, I was sitting with my back right up against the window. People passing outside had their heads level to my bum. This caused much amusement to the bored inhabitants of Boston, standing behind me pulling faces and pointing at my fat sweaty bum. It must have been a sight, what with my T-shirt riding up exposing a deep crack view to the adolescent funsters.

The punk thing as we understood it in the UK hadn't happened in America; being a different culture it never did. The groups over there could all play well. They had done their homework as to being a musician. Yet the punk feel in the UK was influenced by American sounds of Lou Reed, The New York Dolls and others but, like most things in the United States of America, things are packaged more definitively. One of the chaps doing the sound in Boston that night was the drum roadie for Alice Cooper. He didn't really have a handle on what the punk thing was but I was interested to meet him as I liked Alice Cooper when I was younger. A couple girls aged no more than thirteen or fourteen were hanging around as we were getting the gear in. They asked what we were doing. I gave them some badges with the name of the group printed on them; pins as they called them. Later, when playing to a mostly indifferent crowd, I looked over my shoulder into the street and there were these girls, stamping on the badges, then holding them up to me and laughing. I returned my gaze to the people in the bar; some pulling faces which looked as if they were in pain.

The group moved further up north to Canada where we played Montreal. The only thing I remember is telling an Irish joke that fell flat. But it dawned on me a day later that the joke's punch line was based on the theme tune of Match of the Day, a sports programme on television that was only broadcast in the UK. As Howard pointed out to me, they didn't know what the fuck Match of the Day was, it made no sense. I'm not sure if the rest of the Lurker experience did either. The following day it was Toronto. I flew by myself, although scared of flying but it was something to do, although it used up all my money, so, not so good. I'm not sure who the person was but a chap who had something to with prisons or working on the radio, one or the other, approached us and asked if we wouldn't mind signing some sleeves of Lurker records that belonged to this chap who was in prison for murder. This person told us that the prisoner, I don't know his name, liked to listen to our music. He felt that some of the songs could have been written for him, songs of feeling different from the crowd, being scared and wanting to kill and hurt those who upset him. I wanted to visit this person but it would have taken too long to sort out. There were no seventeen year old beauty queens running away from home to meet travelling musicians, no, not for us.

The place we were playing in Toronto was typical of music venues over there. People sat at trestle tables, drinking bottled beer and flipping through menus advertising available food, this being before the advent of that type of thing in the UK. Back home, drink and food was a different experience and in my opinion should remain separate. Back home, food in a pub at night was seen as a hindrance and positively discouraged. A Scotch egg, mouldy sandwich or pasty, constantly re-heated and the customer cursed if any complaint was offered about the freshness of the cuisine. The corporate objectification of designer meals as a fashion statement hadn't yet polluted our society. The serving of meals and the stink of it putting people off their drink was a cultural phenomena I couldn't see working in the UK - how wrong I was. Still, there they were, the audience that is, all denim and shouting clichés. Although it not being in the United States of America, it had many similarities. The guys at the tables banged their bottles, not pleased with the entertainment. This caused Howard to respond with 'negative customer service behaviour'. Being pissed off and bored anyway, he slated the crowd for their Americanness and moaned at them about their heritage and ancestry. "No wonder you left England or your parents did or whoever, couldn't bloody take it, no, you miserable bastards". So it went on. We were 'bottled off' and not for the first time. And it was not the first time that Howard saw it as a victory, meaning having to finish the set early and, when backstage, he would check the beer in his glass and say something like, 'Ah, that's better, saved you lot there, yes boys, you should be thanking me, boring fuckers, get off as soon as possible and have a drink'. He was pleased with himself that we could get off the stage without having to spend forty minutes playing. It was like bunking off at school, getting away with something, as if it was a chore or whatever as he rarely liked the places or people.

Although he did amuse himself by being aloof and I felt at times seeing himself as being a bit clued up on the intellectual front, Howard was most probably more of what he thought he wasn't. I never really connected with Howard although I tried but often found it difficult in his company. I'm sure he saw me as a fucked up buffoon. Thinking about it, he was right about some things. On these sort of occasions the other members of the group just shrugged it off. It was just accepted as him being him and whoever it was in the group who had ruined the night by being drunk or playing all over the place. It was the same thing. There was an acceptance of that person's personality. There was never a band discussion; 'that's the way it is, I guess'. I also remember that in Toronto that night, Nigel brought a young woman back to the room and bounced around in the bed for most of the night. I know it was unusual but I wanted to throw a bucket of water over the two of them. When later reflecting over my feelings, I considered them as being a bit on the Ronnie Kray wavelength of misogyny and odd behaviour.

We drove the van across the border to Detroit. The place we were playing was called 'Bookie's Bar' and we found it deep in a black ghetto. It seemed odd for us to be playing this place. Getting out of the van, we became very conscious of our skin colour. Coming from where we did, this was an unknown culture that was only seen when presented in films. Not knowing what to expect, we started to lump the gear into the bar. It was like many other places that have groups, a bit seedy looking but generally okay. An elderly white bloke sat at one end of the bar and a large muscular black man wearing a singlet sat at the other end reading a book. He nodded to me. I told him that we were playing there. "I know that," he said, showing me the cover of the book that he was reading. It was a book on Greek philosophy. Next to him were a couple of pinball tables. Plug (Pete Edwards) was already having a game. He nodded at me to come over. "Notice anything, erm, different about this place ?" he said, nodding at two white men in tight jeans and white vests who were cuddling each other, one having his tongue down the throat of the other. Plug's eyes then went to behind the bar. The barmen were all white blokes, one was combing the hair of another, all giggled and preened themselves. They wore light green T-shirts with a pink triangle on the front. Plug leant his head closer, "I don't think they're too happy, they saw us getting the gear in and thought we were an ugly bunch. They were expecting something a bit more, well, how can I say, pretty ?" I took a look around the place. It was a gay bar that looked as if it was predominately for white people in a district that looked a no-go area to white people. I wondered how people got there, cab I suppose but then what was I thinking about. What the fuck were we doing there ? This little island of pink mist in a dark sea of discontent seemed at home and I was later told that it was accepted in the area.

I started drinking and found out that the elderly white bloke at the bar was the owner. His name was Bookie, this was 'Bookie'. Bookie had a hole in his throat which was the result of an operation for throat cancer, causing him to make that machine-like noise when he spoke. I could see that Bookie was admired and respected by staff and customers. This was before the gay thing had mass acceptance in the UK, if it has mass acceptance now, I don't know but you know what I mean. Anyway, the place had its own shirt. I was told that the pink triangle is a symbol for progressive thought and an important influence in social change. One of the barmen said he'd give me a T-shirt if I combed his hair. I'm cheap. It was a free T-shirt. He then complained that I didn't have any hair to comb. I gave him a drumstick and told him that was his lot. He turned and told me, "Don't think I have any ideas about you, you're not my type".

All in all, they were a good bunch and meant well. A large white woman with a pasty face turned up wearing shabby ill fitting clothing and a voice that sounded as if it peeled potatoes or gritted the road. It turned out that she was a known lesbian and was also the bouncer. The evening went along and I got talking to a black chap who was a boxer. Now, Detroit at that time was home to Thomas 'the hit man' Hearns, one of the best and his gym was nearby. I got chatting about boxing and about the amount of middleweights that came from this town and then this chap said he'd show me where the gym is that the hit man trains in; a bit of a pattern was emerging about my travels. We left the bar and walked through the streets of the area. It seemed odd walking through a black ghetto.

It was hot and people had sofas and armchairs out on the pavement, they were lounging around, chatting and having a drink with music ricocheting from one portable music system to the other.

"You feel safe ?" the chap I was with asked me, "You're the only pink ass on the street". 'Mm,' I pondered and a police car carrying two white policemen pulled up next to us and drove at our walking speed. I looked at the chap with me. He told me to keep walking. After a few moments, the car pulled away with the policemen looking over their shoulder at us. "They think something's going down," my guide told me, it being an odd sight this time of night in this neighbourhood, a white bloke walking around who obviously didn't come from there. Still, we reached the gym and I did my touching the wall routine, babbling, mostly bollocks, what with the alcohol and adrenaline.

The gig went as normal. There were a few rowdy blokes at the front and behind them stood a semi-circle of the quizzical, indifferent or bored. It ended with a bit of a fight in the crowd but the lesbian bouncer saw to it in no time. So, armed with a bright green T-shirt with a pink triangle on the front, it was farewell Detroit and on to Pittsburgh before our last few days in New York. Still feeling rough from my dose of the near killer Argentinian virus, we returned to the same hotel in New York where the porter continued his chat about Tom Courtney, Burton and Albert bloody Finney. We played Max's Kansas City which I was keen about playing because of its history with the groups that I listened to and all that. It wasn't bad, a bit trendy but okay.

There was a night that we didn't have a gig, so Howard, Nigel and myself went for a walk around and a drink. We decided to get away from the glittery area of Manhattan and try to find a place where *normal* people go for a drink at the end of their day. After wandering for a while, we ended up in an area of Harlem. It was evident from the lack of neon, tourists, grandness of wealth and sell and the shabbiness of this area with groups of young black men skulking along and an old car on its roof by the side of the road, that this Island of New York changed its face faster than a desperate out of work actor. We sighted a bar, 'Jimmy's Bar,' having a neon boxing glove as it's sign. Being out of towner's and plainly not locals, we hesitated in the doorway before entering, only for about five seconds as Howard grunted his impatience at wanting a drink and led the way. The bar stilled momentarily as we entered but soon settled save for the quick checking look. Now, the only person who would go into this bar to cause trouble or want a fight, would be 1: a lunatic (a genuine one, not a supposed one with a lawyer in court) and 2: someone in a Sherman tank with back up outside. We were the only white people in there. It was quite a small place with a lively and friendly buzz. This being 1979, the chaps in the bar all looked like pimps from a Shaft film wearing wide brimmed hats, big lapels on jackets and shirts, medallions and clashing bright colours that glinted in the gold caps on their teeth. Everybody in there looked like Joe Frazier. Thick set shoulders, square on stances and scar tissue was the standard. When I say we were the only white people, we were except for the bar staff which was made up of two white young women dressed in, more or less, see-through leotards with the kind of New York voices that can break concrete. There were no other women in the place. Keeping my eyes fixed to a place called nowhere, I edged to the bar. Howard pointed out to me that under the glass top on the bar counter were hundreds of photographs of boxers, many of them being of one man. I looked up and around the bar. My gaze stopped as it was met by this powerful guy who would have been in his late forties and having the hallmark of an ex-fighter. "Where you guys from ?" he said in a friendly but rather amazed tone. I went through the explanations. He was well meaning as he told us that no white folks came in there. "Hell man, I 'aint saying it's bad, 'an all, it's just the way it is". He went on to tell us that it was a black neighbourhood and it was dangerous but all the same he thought it interesting, us being there and all. He told Howard that he looked like he was in a group but as for me, well ! I said something so obvious it was stupid. I know but in my defence nerves had something to do with it. I said that it certainly seemed like a lot of ex-boxers were in there and was it a boxer's bar. He told me that Jimmy Slade, an ex-heavyweight, owned the bar. He then pointed out Jimmy to me in the photographs on the counter and on the wall. "You heard of him ?" he asked me. "No," I said but went on to tell him that I knew a bit about boxing and that my dad had an interest. He was surprised that I hadn't heard of him. Howard shook his head slowly at me in a way that said, 'Your answer is not the right one, you silly fucker'. All the same, he was a friendly man and we enjoyed a joke together.

There was the odd glance at us but we settled in well. Then I felt a gentle feel on my shoulder that held a great strength. I looked up into the worn but friendly face of a large man. I realised that his thumb was half way down my back and his fingers reached my chest the other side of my body. He introduced himself, this being Jimmy Slade himself. "Hey, you like the fight game ?" He nodded to the guy I spoke to earlier; 'so he had told him,' I thought. My answer wasn't really an answer in the normal sense. It was a frail spewing feeling that had an ancestral meaning to survival. I choked and stuttered until he put me at ease, telling us that he had been to Wembley, quite near to where we came from, just for the night where he knocked out Henry Cooper, very easily by all accounts. He showed me photographs of himself in his fighting days, along with other known people. I phoned my dad, telling him where I was and who I was speaking to. Of course he had heard of Jimmy Slade and he went on to tell me about the man whose bar we were standing in and then I remembered what mad time of the day it was back home.

Jimmy, I'll use his first name in true name dropping fashion, told us that they have a whipround to buy some chicken and chips or fries and he asked us if we wanted to be included and then Nigel became a bit confused as to how much he has to pay, meaning being a bit reticent in paying up. Anyway, a short while later the order arrives, people sit down to eat, Nigel tucks in and there is some query as to whether Nigel had paid his due. Of course, he denied all knowledge of getting away with anything but, typical I thought, people get blown away in those parts for drug deals and the like and we might get in trouble for not paying for chicken and chips. Still, it all went well in the end. It was coming up to midnight, as one bloke pointed out to me by showing me his watch with his face beaming and the place was hushing with a state of expectancy. Tables and chairs were being arranged and people took their places facing a small television up in the corner of the room. We realised something was happening but what we were not sure. The guy who pointed out the time to me said, "Hey, you guys, have you seen this Benny Hill guy ? Christ man, he's the funniest; but he's real naughty". I looked into his wounded face with its flattened nose, eyes that had seen through fear and his broken knuckles on large scarred hands. The man's face lit up and his hands toyed like a child's as he said, "Benny Hill man, he really gets me".

I looked slowly away, a sadness mixed with a kind of poignancy enveloped me but my thoughts changed track as my eyes met one of the girls behind the bar. Chewing hard on her gum, she looked through me as she rasped, "Yeah, the guys love him and he sure is a saucy, what's it". She turned to serve someone quickly before they settled to watch the tele. I watched her and I watched others in the bar, my mind suspended, then woken to the theme tune of the Benny Hill show. Hulking shoulders shrugged self-consciously at the antics of Benny, great fingers pointed, some suppressed laughter behind hands that were hard and had guided and provided in a life that is hard but the rude man turned these men into maybe what we should all be, given the chance, happy and at home with the child that is in us all but from which we are dragged away, in whatever way that happens. Benny turned his face to the camera in an embarrassed, crestfallen way for the last time then chased the un-gettable girl into the distance in the universal appeal of larks performed by the clown. The girls behind the bar were women as they viewed the boys in the bar with eyes half closed to the greater possibilities of our future. And the night was ending for us in that little nugget of life called 'Jimmy's Bar'. One of the guys told us emphatically to get a taxi as it was dangerous not to. We did as we were told.

We were back home and there had been changes happening with our record company and the people around it. I wrote in my diary at the time, 'The management don't seem interested'. Gary Numan and his group Tubeway Army had been number one in the charts for four weeks. Again, the management had got it wrong but, in this case, it paid off richly for them. In their wisdom and great insight they had always thought Gary would do nothing so not offering Gary a recording contract, just a sort of distribution deal. Gary's dad, having a few quid, financed all the earlier endeavours which ultimately paid off, I'm glad to say as I found Gary and his mum and dad to be friendly people. As I've already said, this lack of insight made them millionaires and Beggar's Banquet grew as a record label yet the 'Lurks' had by this time had their fifteen minutes of fame or whatever and I sensed a downhill slide feeling in more than one area affecting the world of The Lurkers.

Why people want to be in groups can be a massive area of debate. It could have something to do with being different, for power, getting women, believing one has something to say and others are interested and want to listen or whatever it might be. Yet, feeling different, and I don't mean in a posey way of standing apart from the crowd but rather in attempting to develop an identity and having something to hide behind, comes closer to the way Pete and I fitted into. It was not an act. It remains, an oddness and loneliness. For those who liked and followed The Lurkers it was obvious. It was in the songs, 'Shadow', 'Be my Prisoner', 'Just Thirteen', 'Freakshow', 'It's Quiet Here', 'Aint Got a Clue' and 'God's Lonely Men'. They were not pieces of music where people had sat themselves down with a plan and route, following a scheme to produce an anthem that fitted the fad. These were heart felt utterances which made it all the worse when meeting many people from the other groups who seemed to have a self, separate from the music that they were playing at that particular time. In a way, it seemed to amplify the feeling of mental illness I felt, of not being up to pace so to speak and always feeling different. There were the groups telling people what they ought to think, like Stiff Little Fingers and many more, giving out a message but I saw it more as a massage as in massaging their egos. Telling people in songs what's needed when in reality it was merely theatre, not the discharge of emotion but mostly contrived. When meeting many from the other groups I often saw them as people who wore the dress, flew the flag, usually with a social message but wanting to be a celebrity and to stand with those a million miles from what their songs purported to represent. Oh yes, the commune commuters changed their trousers and accent, yet their heart still beat to the boring tones of a dull unoriginal culture. Being in a group, to many, is seen as a kind of passport to social adventure. It is common for a person or a group of people to leave where they come from and go to the big city where their ideas might find acceptance and at least not suffer mindless abuse from those that inhabit the place that they're from. As for the 'Lurks', we were from the edge of the big city but found no connection with others that we met in the big city and we were disliked by most in the area where we came from. We were a punk band yet not fitting the ideals of many following punk and we were often sneered at by those in local bands and that's something that continued for years after.

I often found myself defending my group and almost apologising. I suppose it upsets many people if they see someone doing something because somehow they feel that their miserable existence is magnified. In the world of musical mediocrity, conservativeness courses itself though all areas of behaviour and thought. The provincial mind extols the known and safe and its music is played out in stale pubs. Being risky, the weekend rebels groove to the blues rock beat, the groups and their roadies have an affectation of a cynicism about being on the road, yet never have been. There are no threats to conventionality but there is a disliking of those who question their nut shelled homophonic sameness. As a group, we were apart from the pseudo posing, Rock 'n' roll image and the people who inhabited that genre but in the late summer of 1979 Pete's guard dropped, his judgement became poor as he was victim to some ego massaging from what I saw as a snidey bloke called John Plain who played guitar with The Boys. This slimy sod manipulated his way into the group, seeing that the management could also be taken for a ride in giving money for cliché pop rock and a style that fitted the imagination of the parochial minded in rock pubs where cover playing is seen as an art form. From then on, the Lurks' had changed and were set onto an irretrievable course playing mediocre facsimiles of weak ideas.

And so it was. After a few gigs we were off to Paris. I remember my room as being particularly unpleasant. We were staying in the Algerian quarter. The owner seemed to be Chinese, all that's fine but he thought it odd when I asked about the mounds of rat poison in the room and that the sheets were crusty and had pubic hairs littered inside them. Believe me, I don't usually complain about things in hotels, I'm not picky about things like rooms and food but, in this case, I thought it worth mentioning. Pete and Howard had a drinking partner in John Plain. He liked a drink and he liked to gamble. I trusted him as much as I would trust Peter Sutcliffe if you gave him a tool kit and left him in an empty house with a sixteen year old girl who happened to be a dumb prostitute. Still, Pete's drinking increased, so much so that he had ensconced himself in the consecrated ground called his bedroom. Anyway, the upshot is that he nearly died. He hardly ate. I didn't go into his room, it being a place of holiness and all that but was told of his 'illness'. A doctor was called and I entered the room with him, his face screening the boxes of cider and wine that were stacked around the walls and there was Pete, always thin but he looked nearly dead. The doctor took Pete's arm, his face winced at how thin it was and then he surveyed the room once more, taking in the scene. He then looked at me and a couple of other people in the room like we were to blame for letting this thing happen. Holding Pete's arm, as if it was a frozen specimen, he spoke in French to Martin, one of our managers, apparently about the gravity of Pete's condition. He then gave Pete an injection with orders to maintain better health and to rest. Snapping open a window, he looked into the street with a kind of disgust on his face. I went out for a drink. I cannot remember if it was before or after we played the gig but we returned to record a single, New Guitar in Town, it was to be the last recording for me in that phase of 'Lurker life'.

After an attempt at producing a polished sound on the single, it still didn't do very well. After all, there had been established groups playing that stuff for years. We then played a few gigs. We did a Christmas gig with the legendary Slade in Guernsey before playing the Music Machine on the last day of 1979. It was to be the last time I played in that line up. I knew things had changed around the group. My grandmother was being taken to hospital by ambulance as I was arriving home in the early hours of New Year's Day. She was a person that I was extremely close to. For me, it was the end of The Lurkers. I was told that I had a debt of £16,183. Pete made an LP with John Plain and some other snidey fuckers although Plug, (Pete Edwards) played on it and I never held anything against him for doing so. Anyway, it all accumulated a large debt for Pete as the record didn't sell and money was wasted. Being disgruntled with playing in a group, I got labouring work from a bloke in a local pub and a few months later Beggar's Banquet starting sending me nasty letters about wanting the drum kit back. A chap called Mark who I haven't seen for years, worked as a solicitor. He liked the group and, thinking this unfair, he sent them a letter back and that was that. Following that, the taxman was on our backs. We made visits to the tax office but I think the taxmen were more interested in Beggar's Banquet books than the scant pickings from our bones.

Besides cutting grass for shit heads I was asked to play for a local group who I thought were good. We called ourselves The Mint. It wasn't like The Lurkers but I quite enjoyed it. Although, it has to be said, the venture was fruitless due to the demons associated with provinciality.

Arturo asked me to play with a chap he knew by the name of Julian who called himself and his group Aunty Pus. Now, Julian was the son of a headmaster at a private school, a very middle class Jewish boy who wrote and played a disjointed type of sound and couldn't hold a note if it was welded to his hand. But this didn't stop him setting up himself to be ridiculed as he made a name for himself supporting The Damned who relished the activity of abusing and humiliating Julian who suffered this to claim his fifteen minutes. Julian had people playing with him who I'm sure weren't too sure why they were, albeit he is a good character, so I suppose that suffices. The usual line up was Robin Bibi on guitar, Dick Taylor on rhythm guitar, Dick having been in the original Pretty Things and played in a group with Mick Jagger, Arturo on bass and me on the drums. It was, is, unfortunate that Julian, like many others, had a bad habit yet he has survived and continues to walk the walk every day. Although, I did wonder what else he might have achieved had he been living his life free from the effects of his habit ?

Having earned a bit of a name for himself playing as a support to groups like The Ruts and The Damned, Julian strove to get his own gigs and it has to be said that most of them were pretty bleak. One of the grimmest was a day we spent hanging around the back of either the Music Machine or the Electric Ballroom, both places being in North London. It was a miserably cold and wet Sunday, the dressing rooms were damp and freezing and in an outhouse not having an ounce of comfort or warmth, a characteristic shared with the people concerned who were running this gig. A chap called Howard played drums in Art's group at that time. He was hanging around with us whilst we waited to do our supporting act. I can't remember who was headlining but anyway, Howard was about five feet six inches tall and weighed about eight and a half stone, his humour had a way that could come over as a bit sarcastic. One of the security or bouncers who weighed about twenty three stone took a dislike to Howard's quips. I recognised the bouncer as being one of the security who were present at The Lurkers' gig at Brunel University a few years earlier and he was very heavy handed. As we were sitting in a dismal dressing room, this particular bouncer came in and gave orders concerning the structure of the proceedings in a manner one would imagine used by a piece of fuckshit organising a dog fight. Howard made a quip and the bloke stopped in the doorway staring at Howard as his brain went through the few revolutions needed to shake up his four brain cells as they struggled for a response. He pointed at Howard, went to say something but didn't, turned and exited. As we all looked at one another in relief, the door opened with a bang and the bouncer bloke returned. Walking towards Howard with a fixed stare on his face, he was holding a large cooking apple. We all sat and watched as Howard shrunk into his chair and this bloke placed the apple on top of Howard's head then smashed his fist down onto it, pulverising the apple and Howard dropped into the chair almost knocked out. The bouncer bloke turned, checked around the room as if it was a job well done and left.

I found myself being bored for most of the time and this would increase my drinking and ranting at people. Being paid nothing, I was there mainly for the drink which I had to buy of course. One night down the Music Machine, Arturo counted that I had drunk sixteen pints before we went on and about another five afterwards. The drummer of the group that we were supporting let me use his drums. I remember him as being a miserable sort of bloke. Anyway, after we played, I think he wanted to beat me up because I had waded into his kit with such fired up gusto.

Life with Julian did leave some interesting images though. On one of the gigs we were playing a support. It was a big gig. It might have been The Music machine or The Electric Ballroom. Anyway, the promoter's wife showed incredible sensitivity to nasty behaviour, not liking foul language and the like. After all, as was explained by one of the bouncer lackey types who was a piece of plankton in the ocean that her husband owned, she was a 'lady'. She seemed to be dressed for an opening of a criminal's bar in the Spanish coastal area where the official currency is swagger, fear and violence. She walked around the gig during the sound checks, listening intently with condescension as one of her husband's men gave her a guided tour, her chunky gold jewellery reflecting in the concrete-like sheen of her permed hair. It being a Sunday, there were orders for everyone to respect her pious beliefs; after all, she was a 'lady'. Julian thought this funny so he got a personal warning to behave. Anyway, Julian stayed backstage as the rest of us started up the set waiting for him to make his entrance. On he came, dressed in a mini skirt, fishnets and jackboots. Waving to the crowd, he got his dick out and started to mime having a wank. Seven seconds later one of the gentlemen from security ran across the stage, grabbed Julian by his neck and dragged him off. I believe Julian got hit by a couple of the *re-directive* officers who 'counselled' Julian and explained to him how upset her Ladyship was, what with her fragile disposition and all that. That was that, for the night. The sight of Julian in his mini-skirted outfit seemed to anger some people and in front of five hundred skinheads representing different National Front and British Movement factions, one wouldn't get odds for there not being an aggressive response to Julian's style and presentation. As was the case at another gig where there was a particularly hostile mood and it was going to be hard going from the start.

Crowds of skinheads from North and South London were ready to clash at the front, as I say about five hundred I suppose. I spotted Chris Henderson, flailing about at the front, giving orders and revving up for a bit of ultra- violence so to speak. Needless to say the atmosphere was grim and not conducive to having a bit of light-hearted banter, a bit of self-ridicule and generally having fun. No is the answer to any such thoughts. The crowd was just about to start fighting each other as we went through an introduction, waiting for Julian to make his entrance. Now, to set the scene, most of the crowd were there for violence, rightwing slogans were being chanted maliciously and, at this pop concert, the unity of the crowd was displayed by raising their arms to do some 'sieg heiling' rather than holding up candles with one hand whilst holding the hand of the person next to you. I can't really explain Julian's, well, stupidity. Here he was, obviously Jewish with his curly black hair and black rimmed spectacles, speaking in a poncy posh accent and how would he approach this situation ? Well, he marched out in his mini-skirt, boots and blouse, kicking his legs in a grotesque Nazi style of march, giving the 'seig heil' salute and shouting into the microphone with a camp lisp, something like, "Oh, hello you big rough boys, I bet you would like to meet a nice Jewish boy like myself ?" The effect was like raw meat and piranhas in a small tank. I was lucky not to have had my head knocked off by the amount of bottles that were thrown with savage anger. Ten seconds later, I was backstage holding a pint of beer and my favourite cymbal.

When not playing with Julian, I played in a group called True Life Confessions for a while. John Dummer and his wife Helen ran the group. John played in the group Darts, Harry played in Squeeze, Robin Bibi who played with Julian was on guitar and two black, french young women (I've forgotten their names) sang with Helen. The group was based in New Cross, South London. John was a bit of a scallywag as are many that scheme and move in the world of popular music. We did a couple of singles but it didn't come to much. The group had a burlesque theme and was a bit knockabout, each of us having a little act of our own. Mine being a parody of a stand-up comedian, not that restful on the nerves when nearly every gig played was a shabby pub in South London. It was the time of the riots in the early 1980's. One evening, we were playing in a pub down the Stockwell Road leading into Brixton and the police had built a barricade right outside the doorway to the pub, making my exit a little difficult as I tried to leave carrying my snare drum.

This bloke, Richard, who wrote the music for The Rocky Horror Show, produced a single that the group recorded. John knew him. Maybe he thought a little of Richard's success might rub off on his new venture. Anyway, this Richard booked the group into a studio in Eastbourne. It was run by Young

Christians or something like that, all wearing chunky jumpers and sandals. The studio was a bit of a holistic God Complex having accommodation in which we stayed for a couple of nights. It was real rock 'n' roll man. We slept in a dormitory having bunk beds. There was a no smoking and a no-drink policy. The group wasn't a druggie bunch but if there were any ideas of that kind of thing I'm sure that one of the chunky jumpered, Young Christians with the trademark washed smile would offer counselling. This was possibly the most memorable thing about playing in that group.

Life with Julian brought me into contact with Young Christians of a different order. An exceptionally grim night was spent playing a gig in the Blue Coat Boy, a pub that was in The Angel, North London. It was a known haunt of the skinheaded. We were a broad church and Julian was such a desperate bastard, he, like many others, would turn up anywhere if asked to do so. So, we arrived one summer's evening on a Sunday. The pub had just the one drink on sale, lager. That didn't bother me but it was a strange scene, just lager taps with no bottles of spirits or wine. A few of the skinhead girls were sitting on the counter. One of them was a member of the bar staff. She did not get up to serve me but just leant across the bar, poured the drink, gave it to me and held out her hand for the money, chewing gum all the while with eyes that appeared to be lifeless. The place was a sea of Union flags, capped sleeved T-shirts and bad atmosphere. The doors of the pub were open and a bunch of disco *cum* soul boys, the typical straight-back yobbo type, came walking by the pub. Words were exchanged with a mob in the doorway and a fight broke out. It was a particularly vicious affair and there was no escape and nowhere to hide. "Who wants some ?" shouted one of the disco types after they had got the better of the skins. Nobody took up his offer. The singer, Ian Stuart, of the notorious skin group Screwdriver, was one of the skins in the doorway. I saw him get whacked, turned upside down by two of the straight-backs and then smashed down headfirst through the glass top of the jukebox. They were a rough bunch. Ian Stuart was helped out of the jukebox. He was bleeding a fair bit and someone gave him a new T-shirt as his other one had been ripped from his body. He recognised me as he was putting on the new shirt and said, "Hello Esso". I asked if he was alright and he shrugged and whined in his Northern accent, "Yeah, oh yeah" as if it had just dawned on him what had happened and he said, "Don't worry about that, we'll deal with it. Yer still playing the drums then are yer ?" He went on quite unconcerned with the incident. It was a grim gig. Another one with plenty of 'seig heiling' in a charged atmosphere as the skins had rallied their troops expecting the fun bunch to return after a night of waltzing to Luther Van Dross or whatever.

This was the time of 'Oi' music and one of its influential supporters, before evolving as a family values man in the media, was Garry Bushell. The violence and aggression at some of the gigs got me down. One night in Norwich (I think we were supporting Max Splodge), a fight broke out. I was standing next to Gary Bushell and I thought he liked what was going on. Gary is not a stupid bloke but he liked the boisterous lad thing. I looked around myself and thought, 'what the fuck am I doing ?' Playing with other groups didn't feel comfortable. I felt locked in my bubble, always feeling on the outside and I felt a lot of it was on the tail end of hippydrome. I saw myself being dragged into situations and going along with things I had never done before. I remember on one occasion that Julian was crawling around some old bag who was acting as an agent or promoter for a grubby gig in some pub. I'd had a drink, said what was on my mind and was reprimanded for it, being told it was difficult to get gigs and that you had to butter people up. I couldn't give a fuck. It was something I had never done, it wasn't the same and it didn't have the neurotic, homely world of The Lurkers. We had our honest felt message whilst this was a world of replication and social competition. I was meeting a lot of wankers on the make and my heart was not in it. I felt that I was only asked to come along because of The Lurkers having a bit of a name in that area of music and there I was, often feeling that I was being pushed into line for expressing my individualistic view. It was not to last.

Trois

Around this time, it was early 1982, Pete (Stride) wanted to do some stuff after Mike Stone had approached him. Mike had established himself in the Stoke area. He ran a record shop and had a label going called Clay Records. Beggar's Banquet had no plans for Mike. Other people joined the company and they were advanced but Mike was held back, remaining in his place working behind the counter in a shop and yet it was his ideas that built up the record label. Anyway, he moved north, got married and started his own thing. The stuff on Mike's label was predominately 'thrash punk' with groups like Discharge. The grunge/squat, Dick Shit and the Razor culture had seized the punk thing and the festivals returned, we didn't and would never have played such things. The open air, rock 'n' mud weekend; the thought induces nausea. The Lurkers were not of that scene, making songs that screamed of imminent world destruction to a backdrop of industrial generators. It didn't sound like rock 'n' roll. It was heavily identified with Mohican haircuts, a pose of urban decay and with a constant threat of Armageddon yet all the while having a heavy feel of the system's presence, as if being controlled with guidelines, like having a procedure and policy involvement of social workers whose mission statement was having an awareness to the kids and the societal implications of mental health. There were those doing gigs in squats, a little like the hippy commune culture of a decade before and now it had returned with an urban setting having a social conscience. Where the fuck would The Lurkers fit in with all this ? We didn't. Pete, Nigel and myself got together and auditioned for a singer. It took place in a converted works unit in an industrial estate just outside Uxbridge. Not many came forward and what with us being useless at doing this sort of thing, inertia was setting in but Marc Fincham saved the day.

Marc seemed to like us and he had energy with his own style. He was a bright bugger, about four or five years younger than the rest of us. Having done his A Levels, he had moved to London from Luton with plans of being in a group. He is the sort of bloke who they say is an achiever. A bit pushy for us barren boys from suburbia but it was most probably what we needed. Now, Marc was camp, he played that game, he posed about in very camp fashion and flirted with the idea and image of being the ostentatious queer who could pack a punch. Mike Stone was pleased to get the group back together although I must say his primary focus was with Pete rather than the rest of the group but that's okay as he saw that it was Pete who wrote nearly everything. Although Pete, Nigel and myself weren't what could be classified old at this time but it wasn't the same; at times there was the feel but essentially it felt more objective and now there was a crossover with other influences as the original punk sound had marbled its effects throughout popular music.

So, we 'hit the road' feeling self conscious but off we embarked on our voyage with a chap called Mick Brewer who was a friend of my brother doing the driving and running around. Tongue in cheek maybe but, to give Marc his due, he went for it with all he had. And what he had was a bit of a put off for some. The grunge/thrash etcetera army was now seen as punk, so Marc in his make up and glitter boots ruffled a few feathers in the mohicans of those who did not understand or like the influence that The New York Dolls made to punk music. Anyway, bollurks to them all.

We recorded two singles, 'This Dirty Town' and 'Drag You Out'. An LP was later released of stuff we had done in a studio. The first single, 'This Dirty Town' was recorded in a studio in Birmingham. It was a forty eight track studio and the sound was the worst the group ever had. It was useless trying to talk to Mike Stone about it. He would never listen to me. He had pigeon holed me as mad fucker in that indomitable Northern way of seeing humour. The studio was hi tech and modern in having toys and gadgets for people to play with as well as a pool table and television. The bloke that ran it was a hippy type and I saw his lady as one of those hippy types who make out that they are gentle people. The snare drum sounded like a ping pong ball being thrown by a sickly three year old girl against the boarded window of a workman's hut in a force eight gale. No matter what I said, it wasn't listened to and I was hitting the thing so fucking hard my fingers and nose bled. So, that was me pissed off. The lady of the studio had a sideline in doing food, carrot cake and frog sperm drinks, that kind of thing. Needless to say, when I mentioned going to the chip shop, her face screwed up in repugnance as she went on about toxins. She saw herself as very precious. So much so that later on, as I was watching the television, she wafted in the room wearing the obligatory long sexless dress that the hippy type wear and spoke in her middle class monotone the sensitive words, "They've killed another Argie". This was the time of the Falklands War. I was living in a country where people were defying their expected social roles. Sweet, innocent-faced little girls were crayoning battle scenes under the guidance of church-going, Christian, primary school teachers and donating their favourite picture to be pasted on a bomb so it could be dropped on the Argies. When standing in pubs, it was not uncommon for estate agents or teachers to rush in and announce to people news of the killing. Secretaries would greet customers with news of our boys and of 'they've got some more; it's going well'. The country was at war. It was two years before 1984 but I was already feeling a bit like poor old Winston Smith.

And here, in a dark studio, the purveyor of non-aggressive food and selfish interests was adding her poisoned penny to the bill. I asked if she had thought who the Argies actually were and maybe they are the same as our lads and they're all being used. But I was living through a time when reason was shifted as an obvious and clumsy propaganda weaved its web. The Falklands War was playing in some soap set in a place that wouldn't hurt anyone important. A war creation designed by lesser individuals who pursued power and people showed their brutish, cruel, narrow colours with pride. The Argie was there to be despised and everything we did not know about them. It was an exercise in a collective ignorance and negative response. Our would be unemployed fighting with other poor people, for their lives, the only thing they have, in quagmire hell; all orchestrated by those who have always had the three numbers that rhyme with dicks branded on their necks. I told her to stick her peaceful and kind cuisine. The laid-back, liberal voice of the new, laissez faire, hippies with their really nice music and having values having pretensions of being alternative were in fact as alternative as cleaning one's teeth twice a day. They gave a full consensual nod at total conformity but held on to a fabricated façade of being caring. Her husband came in, so I told him my thoughts and then Mike Stone said I should I apologise as I had upset her. I told Mike to piss off out of it. The only thing that upset those types is if you did them out of money or they felt they were missing out on something and there wasn't ever much chance of me turning over hippy slime ball types, they had it honed to perfection. Still, happy days. We took the bag of shit of a recording and 'hit the road'.

Marc was confrontational which was good but it had its bad side when mixing with violent bastards. Most of the gigs we did were rough and Mark camped it up more as the aggression rose. I don't think it was a conscious thing to provoke people, it was just his way of dealing with it but even so, it was self perpetuating.

It was 1982 and the country was going through a shake up. It was like watching a tape on fast forward as a post industrial crumble was unleashed on the towns and cities. Whatever the motives of the State, it seemed like a war; one only had to venture out of London and even the partially sighted would witness the challenge that was placed in our society. Middlesbrough is a good example. We played there a few times as the original group and then with Marc. The closure of workplaces, the uncertainty, the fear and suspicion that accompanies insecurity was etched through this place. The Rock Garden was a gig positioned within ring roads, urban decay and the flinching, twitching of poverty; a condition often imagined to exist elsewhere in some other country. I was skint and didn't look as if I had money yet was warned in a pub to watch myself by a chap when I went to the toilet as I was seen to get a five pound note out of my pocket. The bloke nodded to a table. There sat a small group of men staring at me, resentfully, in the type of grey overcoat attire students wear for an experiment but this was for real. Places of work had shut down. The sight of strangers with London accents aroused attention and I felt the anger.

The gig itself was always a rough one to say the least. That particular night was going to be that type of night when things would go wrong and you hoped it wouldn't end in a total disaster. Quite often, well nearly always, one of the group played terrible, due to being drunk mostly but this evening everyone seemed rubbish, most of us were drunk. The crowd was hostile. There wasn't many there but enough for bad feeling and a fight. It was obvious that there was dissatisfaction towards the group and the grim atmosphere got worse. The experience ended with us fucking around and the stage getting invaded as the crowd had a mock fight as if they were joking with us but they were really taking the piss and being nasty. So, that was it, another night in rock 'n' roll twilight world coming to end. When packing the gear away, we discovered that a drum, a cymbal and Nigel's amplifier had been stolen. The bloke that ran the place was from the London area and seemed a bit of hood type of bloke. Anyway, he wasn't happy. He said he wouldn't pay us as he hadn't taken enough money on the door and that a cheque would be in the post. He moaned about people complaining and was surprised by our show, especially from a group that was supposed to have a bit of a name and people had paid to see them. The feeling all round was not good. A week or so later we got a letter from the London wise promoter, owner or whoever he was. It set out an explanation of why he wasn't going to pay us. Now, this letter was a gem and I wanted to keep it because it was funny as hell. I can't remember it word for word but it had the feel of building a letter, like a child trying to sculpt clumsily with tools that are too large for the job. It was an attempt at being professional to avoid payment. The place was a shit hole and there was always a fight in the place. The letter read like, "the cheque is withdrawn, punters got upset and started fighting because the group was shit. I have never seen or dealt with such unprofessional people, I have never heard such a row in my life," etc. Another satisfied customer.

Yet that wasn't the last we heard from our evening in Middlesbrough. A few weeks later the police sent us a letter from Stockton police station, just by Middlesbrough, saying that they understood we had played at The Rock Garden and had some equipment stolen and that they were pleased to inform us that it was at the station. What had happened was that a bloke had come to the gig, jumped on stage at the end and with the help of his mate nicked our stuff and got it out of the place. Being drunk or just doing it for a laugh, he chucked the gear over a fence into a little hiding place that they knew. Well, the police found this out because this bloke who had nicked our stuff had written a letter to his brother who was in prison down in London. Apparently, all letters are read through and there it was, in the bloke's own hand, divulging his night of fun and plunder. The prison staff informed the police up in Middlesbrough who, in turn, went round this bloke's house, nicked him and got the gear back. We told the police that although the bloke was a bag of shit we weren't in the business of pressing any charges but the law dealt with him anyway. They told us to collect the gear by a certain date or it would be auctioned off for the police orphan fund; yeah, I bet. Needless to say the stuff wasn't picked up so I suppose some son of a copper ended up with a bit of kit to help him on his way.

The first of the two singles we recorded with Marc had a good review from Garry Bushell who then worked for Sounds. I must say, it was good of him because he knew probably more than ourselves that The Lurkers were not a hip outfit and not that cool to associate with. Although we weren't part of the 'Oi' movement, he took the time to invite us up to the paper's offices where he played the single on a fragile looking little record player. By the looks given from other staff, he was doing it to wind them up or prove a point. But, all the same he did. I spoke briefly to Garry about the 'Oi' fashion and of that night he came to Norwich and the trouble involved but he was, is, a bright bloke and knows his way around the media machine. Our second single, 'Drag You Out', followed a few months later. It was big on chorus and big on camp; it didn't fit and we didn't fit. We did not relent, evangelically taking our message to the towns and places of populace in this great land. One day we arrived in my favourite place for lunatics, Bradford.

The place we were playing was quite a small gig and in a rough area. After setting up the gear and going through a couple of songs, Marc and myself went off in search for a pub. As I said, the area was rough, a bit no man landish, in what seemed like waste land, maybe ready for development amongst ring roads and between the shells of the few uninhabitable small terraced houses. A pub stood on the corner but on first sighting appeared closed or shut down as the windows were boarded up and oddly the whole place was painted black, giving it a bit of a surreal mood in it's desolate urban setting. We went up to the pub to inspect it further for any life. It was in fact open. We could see life or at least light between the battened boards covering the windows. I tried the door; it was open. Being a couple of cowards, we shuffled around each other as each one didn't want to walk in first. After all, if it was a real 'blood letting centre' walking in next to Marc with his painted nails and straw boater hat, well, it could be dangerous. Marc said, "You go in first and I'll walk casually behind you". 'Ah, sod it,' I thought, 'lets get a beer'. We got to the bar and ordered a drink. The barman turned to get them and, as I was thinking he gave us a bit of a long look, I noticed a water jug on the bar used for mixing with whiskey. It was the shape of a penis. Very surprising and what a find for Marc, he could preen himself, strut around and generally show off. I can't remember if we outstayed our welcome but we left telling a couple of the locals that we were playing the gig nearby. This raised smirks of distaste at the very thought of going there.

Back at the gig the place was full with a bunch at the front who were a mix of skins and regional hard nuts. A thought of canvassing to raise funds to build a local Woman's Centre to explore marginal sexual preferences and proposals to book a gypsy Peruvian nose flute group crossed my mind. Why ? I couldn't tell you. The promoter was a chap who was older than we were, maybe in his mid-thirties, having a cropped balding head, a donkey jacket and a precise and soft Northern accent. He seemed politically 'right on'. He had a friend who was a seventeen year old of Pakistani origin. He looked like a cross between an Elvis look-alike and a punky art school type. He weighed no more than seven and a half stone and spoke in a broad Bradford accent that was camp with aspirations of wanting to sound tough. His speech and actions were melodramatic and, when he and Marc clasped eyes on one another, it was something like a showdown in a Bollywood musical. They were barely introduced as the Asian Elvis flitted into his Brando On The Waterfront scene, brushing Marc's hand away as he went to shake with him and demanding to know where we had been and that there had nearly been a riot and what did Marc consider himself to be, "professional, or an amateur ?". From then on it was flashing eyes, twisted mouths, gritting teeth and knotted fists, standing face to face shouting at one another, the only thing missing was twelve full length mirrors for them to watch their performance in. Their titanic clash continued as we made our way on stage, fingers pointing, cursing accusations and threats. It was so sudden and wrathful, well, it was bewildering.

We lurched into the set yet within minutes the brown babe Bradford rock 'n' roller was on stage, clearing a microphone lead away or putting a microphone stand in place, all the time managing to edge Marc with his elbow, sneering at him, as if Marc's incompetence needed his skills. Marc shouted in New York tones of voice to, "Fuck up off out of here," then raising his finger towards him. The Bradford Bomber threw himself backwards, landing on his back, pointing up at Marc with threats. He then got to his feet and aimed a punch that travelled no more than six inches, had the power of a sick kitten stretching a yawn and was about six feet away from Marc but yet, Marc reeled across the stage as if being hit by a low flying missile, screaming in pain and rage. And so the fight continued. We would play for half a minute and then another vicious brawl would break out, complete with threats of staggering intent. Nigel turned and looked at me, still playing. He shrugged and offered a bemused smile. Pete also turned, looking at me, his face incredulous but secretly loving it. I watched the gang at the front. At first they shouted at Marc to get on with it but they eventually stood and watched. They were astounded, some with arms folded and disbelief on their faces. The hardest task after the gig was keeping the two highly charged adversaries apart as the words of war swung from threats of physical harm and death to whining comments on looks and clothing. The promoter was embarrassed about it but to me he appeared to have accepted his lot and continued in his neutral manner, saying he knew of a curry house that is open late. We were staying around the promoter's house that night so, with the gear packed in the van, the promoter jumped in with us and off we went, leaving the 'Asian Bradford Bomber' on the pavement, in the rain, sulking as he didn't want to come. We pulled away, Marc making threats to him out of the window.

After a plate of Hiroshima sauce, bread and a couple of drinks, we drove under instruction from the promoter to his house. The rain beat down with a ferocity that made me wonder if the nearby Pennine hills were breaking apart but it was nothing to the implacable rage held in the heart of Marc's sparing partner when we arrived. We pulled up outside the house and there he was, a pathetic form, as if trapped within the dark dripping terraced housing. He wanted no shelter from the hard rain, his show was of suffering, wretched and drowned, soaked through to his precious skin he stood in the middle of the road, his lonely figure embedded against the street light. As we were getting out of the van, the suffering one launched into the promoter, "What's he doing here ?" pointing at Marc who snubbed his nose at him. A couple of us told them pack it in. The suffering one simpered sulkily to the promoter, "Look at me, I'll most probably get pneumonia and die." The promoter bloke had a long night ahead of him.

I never did like crashing at people's houses. I'm miserable I suppose but I hate that rotten feeling when not having much sleep, the booze still whirring away in the head making the nerves clang throughout the next day and sometimes bumping into people in the morning who live there but you didn't meet them when you had bludgeoned in during the night and were given cushions to make a bed on the floor. No, not my thing and it never was. Anyhow, on this particular evening I was given privileged treatment. Available spaces on sofas and floors were arranged. Then the promoter told me that he had a sort of attic room which he knew I would like. The room was tiny with a sloping ceiling, making standing impossible. The promoter bloke had put a little electric fire in there. He then went about setting up a small radio, telling me that I could listen to the World Service, "And be cosy and warm, I knew you'd appreciate that."

And there it was, The Lurkers, second time around. We went on to record some more stuff and work on an LP but it didn't come to much. Pretty soon it would be the end of something significant to me although I didn't realise it. It was at that time that The Lurkers finished as being 'The Lurkers' and all that made it so. The name has been presented on stage and toured but the feel and all that it embodied and meant had been spent way back then. Marc was a bright bastard. He's married with kids as far as I know. He didn't think that I was a group type of person. Maybe he was right but what I do know is if he tried it on with other groups who had been given a slice, albeit a thin slice, of the cake, he would have been told to bugger off. But he entered 'Lurker Land'; it did not matter if you could play well or sing well, the requirement was to have an understanding to the unwritten philosophy of it all. He gave us a kick up the arse but it was too late, money was cut and he grew out of it or it just ran its course for him. He started talking and comparing us to Kadgagoogoo or whatever they were called. Madness is accepted in 'Lurker Land' but there are limits; finish.

During the years I have remained a friend with Arturo. We went on a holiday a week before Christmas in 1982. We went to Leningrad, basically to see if they celebrated the festival and had Christmas trees. It started from a bet I waged down a pub that Russians celebrate Christmas. They did and it was bloody cold. Art and me did sod all there. The trip was full of Guardian-reading, art enthusiasts.

Arturo has always had one or two things on the go. His group, The Blubbery Hellbellies, were starting around this time. I played drums on the first LP. Art and me are good friends but it doesn't work playing in a group together. His sister Wendy was in the group The Boothill Foot Tappers. It was country type of revival but my mind was elsewhere. I wrote a couple of plays. Not having any training or going to the theatre, I saw it as emotional flu, unclogging those feelings that burn and warp. I had got to know Leigh Heggarty and his mate

Andy Peart, a fanzine writer. Leigh's mum typed up a play of mine. The writing was personal and I liked it, this I did whilst doing labouring work for friends. The punk music thing for me had gone although I went to see the Ramones and went back stage. Joey seemed a very sickly figure. They were rack n' roll, maybe its best to have your imagination and fill in spaces as one sees fit. The 'ligging' and all that goes with it just leaves me cold. Someone gave me some heroin. I put it in a little water and drank it. The woozy feeling gave way to the warm low buzzing rush and I found all that I could talk about was the suffering of young men in the First World War.

A few times in my life I have witnessed terrible acts of fawning which disgusted me and in a way explained the disgrace in the human condition. The worst time was with a bloke I knew in the early eighties who was trying to get a 'tape magazine' together. I went with him to see the group The Thompson Twins. There was a journalist from The Daily Mirror there and the way that bloke spoke to members of the group was so sickeningly sycophantic that, as I say, I saw no future for human beings. Anyhow, I know it isn't just in the media or the music business that the behaviour of humans has shown me why I like my cat so much.

During that period in the eighties and especially around London's suburban area, people like builders became a significant personality in measuring the ethical standard. Many of these types seeing themselves as a throw back to medieval princes, the free beast, might is right, the politics of immediacy; bullying and taking 'because you can' predominated. This being before the age with its fashion for mobile phones. When entering a pub, the chief builder would place his van keys on the bar as a territorial statement, behind him standing in servility were his men. The sloganeering provided by the media was simple and directive. The years of struggle as waged by Chartists with their principles for reform, the involvement of the church and unions in efforts to create fairness and some kind of egalitarian basis for an individual to have worth is lost on this mob. From miserable experience, I can vouch that I know the type of people who would volunteer if the State wanted to hire people to hunt down and interrogate innocent people, if they were deemed weaker than they were and against their ways. I will give a small, yet not uncommon and certainly not extreme example of the guiding philosophy prevailing within the ranks of the suburban Princes.

They have aspirations of expressing a cavalier presentation and a cheering of fair play if someone achieves something, even if it is at someone else's expense although this attitude is not directed universally, it is reserved for whom I call the bullies of the world, meaning people like themselves. There is a doffing of cap for the powerful, at first sighting at odds with a seemingly rugged individualism but theirs is a mixed philosophy having a blind reverence to the paternalist overseeing stately figures who, I suppose, are the biggest thugs of them all. These free beasts, I found, who shout and growl their independence of a society, appear to be the first to cry if there are no hospital facilities if one of their offspring falls ill but that's the way it is I suppose.

Anyway, getting back to my example. One evening, after finishing a day's labour, the chap I was working with dropped into one of the local pubs. In this pub there would be a gathering of builder types having a drink before going home. The pecking order is clearly defined and the sway of conversation dictated by the paymaster. Someone usually has to suffer if a demand or wanting of some kind is not being met. On this occasion a particularly aggressive prince stood with his back to the bar. He struck the common pose in this social circle which is to roll one's neck, have arms folded, legs apart with the bollocks being frisked and nose cleared between every other sentence. He was venting his annoyance and his men stood in deferential poses, similar to their leader. His subject for that evening's grace was that he and his men had been working down in South London all day and he'd 'gone into one' because they had seen "wogs, paraffin lamps and nutters and none of the cunts wanting to work". His men nodded in mutual support as chief prince gave his reason for his consternation. It transpired that he was going on a driving holiday to Italy with his wife and one year old daughter. His concern was that, apparently, he had been told that safety checks on child seats for the car were varied, he had been told there were different brands and it was up to him to make a choice. There was muttering and shaking of heads from his men but always keeping one eye on their master. He then launched into his concluding tirade, telling of thoughts that he had that afternoon whilst in his van. "It's been doing me fuckin' head in, fuckin' cunts, I smashed me hand on the dash and says to the men, look at all these cunts walking about here, not even fit for starting fires with, why can't the cunts running the country who are meant to have the brains, use these cunts to test the safety of the car seats on, put these cunts to some fucking use." He finished and, turning in disgust, he picked up his drink. His men nodded, looking from one another, pondering the great insight and wisdom shown by the irate prince.

It was summer and had been a hot day. It was in this weather that they seemed to come into their own. It often struck me as a kind of colonial type of culture with leisure interests being golf, getting properties in Spain and only having an interest or understanding of things. I often imagined that a chip of South Africa had blown away and embedded itself in the London Borough of Hillingdon.

This was their world, a physical world, resenting constraints of the other world, that being the rest of society. Seeing themselves as separate, even a distinct beast from the puny and weak suited office worker type where work was a world inhabited by women and it was seen as women's work. Whilst their own world was known and controllable, partners in business or labourers were those known, even from school days and usually known in the pub. It was a small world, safe and predictable, run on the lines of the school playground as is the rest of the world I suppose when one thinks of the bullying methods involved in the tactics of foreign policy by large countries. Although, I suppose it is because of the obvious brutish behaviour of the princes in gaining their wants, it at least, in a way, makes them honest when measured against the sneaky methods of certain others, those working in institutions and politics, hiding deceitfully behind a correct language and creating an industry from the hardship of others as they plan their personal plunder. Yet, the 'might is right' doctrine that is practised through every interaction making up the lives of the princes seemed fertile ground to plant the politics being sown during that period. The distrust and suspicion of something or someone who can't be physically dominated develops an ever decreasing circle of limited consciousness.

Power was demonstratively displayed publicly by the use of physical aggression and principally displayed in the culture of 'weighing a man in' down the pub; being paid that is. Usually on a Friday, the prince would get money from the customer or the bank as work finishes early and everyone goes to the pub. When in the bar, the prince will turn his back to other patrons or the bar staff, pull a wad of notes from his pocket, lick his fingers and count off a number, stop, look up at his man and he would nod at the counted amount and then it would be handed over. The ritual was always done in front of people yet under the guise of secrecy. Of course, you could have got paid in the van, well anywhere but this display was central to the controlling role played by the prince.

Still, it was cash in hand work, there was no responsibility and the people who took me on knew a bit about me, drove me to and from work in their vans and were good to me; so it was.

Nigel is a friend of mine and our lives have followed a shared path and that is something I would have thought unlikely when I was young because we do come from different backgrounds. But we went to the same school, shared the experience of being in a group and I'm sure he followed me into enquiring about doing an Access course. It was one day a week. I was nearly thirty years of age and for three other days a week, I had a cash in hand job at an amusement arcade in Acton. Nigel started the same course, going on a different day and worked in the same amusement arcade a different three days of the week. We knew the bloke who owned the arcade. He had three of them in the Acton and Shepherds Bush area. Needless to say they were depressing places, small converted shops giving refuge to the disparate. In one of the arcades next to South Acton estate, a chap from the West Indies used to regularly sleep behind the counter.

Objectively, it was humorous when, at college, a social science lecturer used to bleat about youth and the city, with all words delivered carefully in that liberal neutrality and of course a patronising condescension which is the giveaway to the real attitude and careerist intentions of these types. We were given the square root of a young person's value system as quoted from research conducted by people who see other people as a product. Their qualitative research didn't match my own when having knives pulled out and the constant theft from the machines. Still, 'as long as I didn't get stabbed' that was my thought, 'I just work here, it's a shit hole, take what you fucking want mate'.

There was a lot of idling in a job like that, contemplating the mad, the lonely, the desperate, whether old, young or clinically ill and sometimes the perverse. I would stand in the doorway and watch life as it offered itself down that part of Acton Vale. I used to watch a man whose actions stayed with me as symbolising maybe the futility of life's existence. I found my thoughts more absorbed when sighting him than any of the theory as understood by our society's formal sages. I would say he would have been in his late forties, dishevelled and disorderly in physical presentation and sad in mind. He would stand about one hundred yards or metres away from a bus stop, waiting anxiously for a bus to appear further down the road. On sighting the bus, his anxiety would increase, tightening and re-tightening the belt to his trousers, he would then let the bus pass him then race after it in a show of attempting to catch it which he never did. On the odd occasion when he reached the stop before the bus because the bus had been held up or whatever, he would gesture to the conductor that it was okay and that he wasn't getting on. But the way and style in which he ran for the bus was frantic. His trousers would loosen to a point that they would sometimes slip down his legs, people would jump out of his way and he would mop sweat from his face, cursing that he had missed the bus. He would then walk disconsolately back to his waiting place further down the road, tutting and desperate at missing the bus, only to turn, eyes blazing and running full pelt to miss another one. It could last for a couple of hours, maybe more. And then, as these things happen, I didn't see him any more, these being the days before Community Care.

The man wore the uniform of the fallen Irish labourer; a dark greyish suit that was battered and tired out, holding many stains and maybe belonged to someone else before him. I would have thought he had come from Ireland from his demeanour, being in that area and I had experience of such things. I would wonder if he came from a small town and where it was. Probably coming from a large family and leaving Ma to make a go of it. There is a lot of bollocks talked of the romance of being Irish as depicted in fiction through books, film, music and advertising. And here he was, mad, the drink, frustration and loneliness being a part of it all and suffering curses that are bestowed upon many of the poor who are vulnerable and working against the odds and often people don't understand that many have been displaced by the dictate of power. Like his suit, he was scarred beyond repair, acting out his obsession of trying to catch a bus and if he ever got on it, where would he have gone ?

At this time I had been going around Pete's place and we were doing a few tunes together. We contacted Mike Stone who was pleased to help out, again. After rehearsing a couple of numbers, we went into the studio. We called ourselves Performance. I liked the song that we recorded. It was a bit of its time with the electronic involvement. The producer had arranged for a session musician to play bass and there he was, it was Paul Fox, the Ruts guitarist. The song did sod all and it was the last time I recorded with Pete. I was off to Essex University in my role as a mature student and of course Nigel went as well. Finishing the same Access course, we got accepted by the same university and our interview was on the same day.

The bloke interviewing us remarked on the remarkable coincidence of us knowing each other for so long and of going to the same school, touring around together in a group and now going there together. 'Together' - I didn't like the ring he put to it. I told him that it was a coincidence and that we both had left our mother's houses that morning and drove up there together in Nigel's car and also we had our eye on a nice little cottage out in the sticks and that my hod carrier friend back home is going to knock us up some nice pink cement so that we can re-point that little cottage when it's ours. Anyway, we got accepted, the rhythm section was off to get edumacated, to read and write - and maybe I would learn to count, a problem when being a drummer. Why ? We didn't know what the fuck we were doing I suppose.

To be a socialist at University, one had to have a haircut like a yucca plant. They have what they call overseas students and I felt like one of them, only it was worse than that as everything and everybody is put in a box and labelled and of course most people love it. In my experience, at that time, what they called mature students was a bunch made up with loads of divorced women dressed in

135

some kind of interesting Amazonian tribal hat and clothing that was alternative from their previous lives. It was as if they were out to prove that bastard of an ex that they were intelligent and that now they were very content, being independent and creating their own life. Neurotic as fuck. Many of the mature students were the thirty something ex-hippy type. Having done the rounds of India, their parents were giving them one last chance to prove themselves worthy of inheriting the family home and all that goes with it. Most of them studied Socialism in Latin America. I heard one of the old dowdy hippy hags calling the cleaning ladies 'crusty old bags' when she saw them waiting at a bus stop. This was in between going to support the plight of the working class who lived in some place in Latin America. The punk background wasn't liked. It wasn't long after this time that punk became diluted throughout the system but I've never been a team player so my attitude set me way aside I suppose.

A known thing in the UK is that it is censorship by class. On my first night at the place I spoke to this right arrogant, weak, waste of space who was a lecturer in literature. When talking to him, he kept adopting a thick, false cockney accent, "is 'at right; nah mate." I should have stuck one on the tosser and yet it did sadden me to think that many people not having the opportunities in life hold many of these fuckers in revered thinking. I didn't fit, needless to say, as many people do not in a place like that and coming from a poorer background, what I saw, confirms preconceived thoughts. I encountered first hand, I suppose, behaviour and attitude I already knew existed. Privilege and all that goes with it; many there had a sheltered existence and not much understanding or empathy with what in the humanities is a large subject of study - the poor. For some, reading Charles Dickens at an early age is as close as they got to being exposed to deprivation. Showing great bravery by just reading it, one needs a little spoiling after such unpleasantness and need to indulge themselves in 'me' concerns and always defending themselves by being busy and rushing from self centring thinking classes to some other 'me' pursuits.

Being in a situation, albeit one I had put myself in, of living with student's after years of taking the piss and moaning about them was ironic. It was as if it came back on me for being such a miserable sod, even though I was usually right in my condemnation. I smiled inwardly, sometimes and thought serves you right, Haynes, when an ex-public school boy of twenty said "it's great living away from your parents, you can have choc ice and chips and mother isn't their to reprimand you." Where the fuck was I ? And what the fuck had happened ?

A student from the USA lived in a house I was staying in. He was like his country's foreign policy in his demeanour and he would talk to me about life and "what really sucks ?" He showed me a photograph of himself at his parent's home. He was wearing a suit and a fancy scarf with a mock rebellious sneer of an expression on his face, at odds with his parent's demands. "Don't you just hate it, look at me, bored, you know the feeling, 'that' feeling, waiting for your parents before going to the opera; what a bummer man." He then laughed in a fashion that emitted little or no noise, nodding at me, as if I knew what the fuck he was on about.

Nigel's experience was similarly grim. He had told the university theatre people that I had written a couple of plays. A bloke called Mark Evans was the Director. He liked one of them and took it to the Edinburgh Fringe where it ran for three weeks. It got good reviews. I went up there but only saw it once. The company did a good job but I wasn't comfortable with that crowd. I spent a week touring the pubs and stayed in the family home of Robin with whom I shared a house during the last year of my degree. Whilst at the university I made friends with Brendan who comes from Belfast. I told him that I had played in a club there and that the place had made an impression upon me. Brendan invited me to his home that was off the Falls road. I discovered a culture of that community with its history and experience apart from and conflicting with, mainstream media presentation. It was of interest and concern to me, liking to get at truth and disliking unfairness. Although I did get the odd thing wrong. One evening I went to a local club that was obviously nationalistic, complete with short haircut, English accent and wearing a red, white and blue jacket. One of Brendan's friends told me later that he didn't have the heart to tell me. But, the seriousness of the situation goes far beyond a matter of the colour of one's coat.

It was 1988, I had about a year to do at university and Arturo had organised getting 'The Lurkers' back together to do a gig in Dusseldorf under the commission of a chap called Campino who is the singer in the German group Die Totenhosen. Campino was a fan of early punk and Arturo had got to know him when playing in Germany with the Blubbery Hellbellies.

It seemed odd, Nigel and me being at that university and rehearsing the old songs. But anyway, with Arturo doing the singing we went and played the one-off gig. It went well I suppose and it gave us another night in Dusseldorf before coming home. We seemed to be split in different hotels. On our night off there was a bit of a party that Arturo, Pete and Nigel went to with some of Campino's friends. I opted to go for a drink in town with a few chaps who had come over for old time's sake, Paul, Paddy and an old friend Colin. I had £110 in my pocket and the idea was to have a couple of drinks and leave it at that. I was skint and needed the money so I put the hundred in one pocket with plans of just having a quiet drink with the remaining tenner. Well, that was the plan. We went to some of the little schnapps bars, started mucking around and that was that. I opened my eyes to find myself lying on the floor in some kind of dance area of a disco bar. And there, on opening my eyes, I saw a bloke sweeping around me with a broom. He was wearing a leather waistcoat, a dickie bow and a large moustache. Looking about myself, I saw Paul, Paddy and Colin sleeping on a bench. It was a kind of gay bar. I checked my pockets, nothing. It was about seven in the morning. We were the only people in there and the place was out in the suburbs. God knows how we got there or more importantly I suppose, why we ended up there. The moustachioed man gave us directions into town. We had a plane to catch in two hours.

It was my last 'Lurker' appointment. Arturo continued with the group with Pete and Nigel playing for a while but then just Art and anyone doing the songs but 'The Lurkers' had long gone.

My days at the university came to an end and I'll leave them with just a final rant or two. It was new to me, seeing the way people allied themselves to the different societies. It was an extension of school and role playing the positions to be filled later in life. The corny patronising way in which politics is dealt with was a cross between funny and annoying. I have since seen some of the characters on the television as community spokespersons or whatever. As a class and type of person, it was all foreign to me. Whether you are a Telegraph or Guardian reader, what does it matter if you live down the same road, drive similar cars and want to send your children to the same school to start it all off again ? There was a lot of talk of bigots and fascists yet I found their dinner table manners with its code of acceptances very opinionated and confined. The barriers are erected and values reaffirmed, their enemy usually being those with limited opportunities, an easy and convenient target. The liberal doctrine has stolen the moral high ground and through advantageous positions set a precedence in the media, education and the arts, thus creating a self reciprocal industry where boundaries of consent are maintained along with the power that goes with it.

So, I left.

The punk influence and its intrusion into mainstream culture has appeared through fashion in many guises. One creation was the emergence of the donkey jacketed, boxing booted, social worker type with short hair and a cockney accent. It was a construction that was cockney but correct yet the giveaway to the hippy monster lurking beneath was a beaded wisp of hair hanging from the back of the neck. It said, 'actually I am not a skinhead'. Then along came other thefts from the skinhead culture like the rucking jacket, also known as the flying jacket and the greatest cultural pillaging of all was hijacking the Doctor Marten boot; 'the boot'. When I was a lad, just the mere mention of a pair of DM's would be the signal for bringing a moral judgement upon the wearer. It was a symbol, being an antithesis to the development of a civilised liberal progressive society. The boot's very existence denoted a type that represented the other and the middle class student type would judge their refinement against the baseness of those who wore this symbol of the enemy. They were an emblem of the skinheads and all that they represented, a sign synonymous with malcontent behaviour with wearers of the boot related to thuggish and evil social activities and having neo-Nazi politics.

They were, in fact, an easy signifier in distinguishing positions within a cultural war. And yet, of course, not everyone who may have been big lumps from working class backgrounds were nasty sods because they wore a pair of DM's and in my experience I have found many of the 'lumpen booted' to have more compassion than the professional liberal types with their 'not in my back garden' ethics. As youngsters, we would tell and hear fables about the origin of the DM, all adding to their specialness and strengthening the bond between wearer and our differences with those in positions of power, usually people from institutions such as teachers and the like. Yet now, the gay social worker wears them with pride to meetings at work and daughters of politicians wear them at university debating societies. The wearer today would be horrified to learn that their DM's were once part of an armoury to terrify vulnerable people. Those occupying minority status were targeted for physical abuse that was frightening, disgusting and causing fatalities. The boot culture had a vernacular of 'paki-bashing' and 'queer-bashing' and often anyone who was an easy prey and had the misfortune of bumping into a bunch of fuck heads out to express their cowardly practices. For the boot boy roamed in packs nearly always attacking when they outnumbered their victim by six or eight to one. Yes, the DM signified fear and revulsion and was often ridiculed with the wearer being seen as having the intellectual ability of a fence post but, most definitely, it was no laughing matter.

And it came to be, in the refectory of an art college, a diminutive young Asian lady wears her size three DM's, cleanly polished to show the pink flake effect in the mauve patent leather. For years, the DM boot has now occupied a cherished place in the more comfortable homes of the middle classes. The wearer may look back with fondness to student days when their trusted DM's carried them through. The DM boot now has a style and an acceptable utilitarian earthiness, their statement is functionalism to frivolous fashion. The boot now has an occupant having a more dominant position in society. It is another cultural acquisition with its past unknown or lost as the modern consumer is obliviously ignorant.

Quatre

I felt that I wanted to be part of society. Why ?

I had finished my degree and went labouring with lunatics again and then I took a course in lecturing people with Learning Disabilities. Well, the disabled people were fine but as for the staff. Anyway, I finished the course with no intentions of working with the *normals* and all their petty, slimy ways. I guess I just wasn't mature enough to deal with all the bollocks. In order to earn a few pounds, I had a short spell of selling roses to bored and desperate motorists on their way home from work. My employers and colleagues had a reputation for, well, let's just say, being able to take care of themselves and not calling in a practitioner from the Court Of Human Rights for consultation when they wanted to settle disputes of any kind. I am a broad church, so to speak, in that I know people coming from diverse backgrounds and all that.

Our patch of horticultural heaven was under the A4 flyover near Chiswick. The business was run by two brothers and their mate would help out who, about a year later, employed me when I did a spot of mini-cabbing for his company. Only just having passed my test, he hired out a car to me as I didn't have one. I didn't do it for long and I'll leave it at that. Anyway, 'Roses. 10 for £3'. I was embarrassed selling them to people, they weren't really roses, well not really at all. To be honest, they weren't roses but little carnation looking things. "Fuck off," was the advice given to me when I raised this fact from my senior in this nomadic retail enterprise who I'll call 'brother one'. 'Brother two' would narrow his eyes whenever I brought up any ethical concerns and watch me as if I had an illness of some kind. Mind you, his customer service skills were singularly survivalist. Knuckle dusters were a common accessory. I was once asked to carry a bag full of the glinting brass babies, ironically they were in an 'Early Learning' bag with a joyous happy face of a child's sweet innocence on the outside of the bag whilst inside a reminder of the inherent contradictions to a progressive path to an ideal world.

On one occasion, a van load of builders, on their way home from posing all day in shorts and T-shirts even though this was darkest November, came slowly by in the long queue of traffic that threaded in clogged lines of fuel emission, all getting trapped under the flyover. Each one of us had a different road leading onto the main roundabout. So, anyway, these builder types were out to take the piss and bully, as is their way. 'Brother two' isn't a physically big person so they saw easy game. The driver grabbed a bunch of roses and threw them into the back of the van to his laughing gang, only for a second later to be smashed in the face with a 'brass people persuader'.

For the most part, it was boring, freezing cold and embarrassing. I am not and cannot fit the part of the chirpy, cockney, cheeky chappy and my doleful feelings most probably showed through. One early evening, I saw the three senior board members having a little pow-wow by the roundabout, every now and then they looked up at me with concerned looks and then, with earnest, returning to their meeting. 'Brother one' disengaged himself from the others and walked towards me in pensive mode, being watched thoughtfully by the other two. On reaching me, he characteristically moved his head to one side, as if what was to be said was in secret and not for prying ears even though we were on the middle of a traffic island and no bugger could hear sod all anyway. He started off by looking me up and down in a considered way before telling me to "Pep up my act as I was putting off the punters". He told me that all he could hear was the electric locking systems clicking shut as the cars reached me. "You're putting off the birds, 'ain't ya ? Scaring them or some fucking thing, smarten yerself up a bit and for fuck's sake, don't look so miserable, you look like an aggressive old man Steptoe. For fuck's sake, you've been on the same bucket for ages."

Actually, it was not true, I had sold nearly as much as they did but to have the opinions of the friendly society in the do's and don'ts of public presentation and what is and isn't acceptable seemed a bit rich. I wasn't banking on the company employing the skills and judgement of corporate psychology and of how to present a positive body language. That being said, he did have a point. The office worker young women did seem to go for the loveable rogue image whilst my grim demeanour and unfashionable clothes weren't engaging in their world. "Oh, sorry if I've offended your company's image," I told him. He told me to shape up and learn by watching him and the other two. I looked over at the other two. They were watching our conversation with grave importance. It was their style of management and control and, talking of control, when it came to territory protection the negotiations were not one that his Holiness the Dali Lama might suggest for compassionate reasoning.

One early evening, a bloke approached me carrying an A to Z London Street atlas. He asked me where it was that we were standing and did I know of good places to sell flowers. This chap was Eastern European and, at that time, there were not many from his part of the world getting into work of this type. Our chat was cut short as 'brother two' called me over and asked what he wanted. On telling him, he told me that he would deal with this. He told the bloke to go with him over to his car. The bloke duly walked with him to where the car was parked. 'Brother two' opened the boot of his car and there was an object resting peacefully amongst the empty wrappings of the roses which I can assure you wasn't a peashooter or a child's water pistol. The bloke reeled back as he was promptly told to "fuck off out it." I don't think 'brother two' ever applied to work in refugee re-location work. It was a shock to me as well when discovering the little persuader resting in the back of the car but hell, that's the exciting thing working with people, the unexpected.

I might not have been a big hit with the girls whilst standing in traffic fumes selling roses that usually weren't roses but, true to my luck, the one admirer I did have was a tall, camp black bloke who looked like he had escaped from the chorus line in a West End musical. He unfolded himself out of a small, old and battered car and asked in a pinched and nasally voice, "Do you sell roses ?" I nodded to the bucket I was holding that had a sign stuck on the side reading, 'Roses, 10 for £3'. "I can't think what I'm holding," I said. He bought some and as he was climbing back into his car I told him it was only £5 for twenty roses. "You people," he laughed, tossing his flowers on the passenger seat as he got in. He threw his head back as if I had made a pass at him and said "A guy can't go anywhere nowadays." He went to say something else but it was too much for him. He drove off or moved along in the queue, wriggling his fingers at me and all the while I heard the electronic clicking sound of door locks as the young women passed me. I looked up. 'Brother one' was watching me, shaking his head slowly.

I wanted to write and so I did, discharging emotional flu. I have had my fair share of signing on and later deemed by the powers as incapable of holding down a job, what with the responsibilities and having to deal with people. I had casual work from time to time and drank a fair bit; where in pubs there are customs that exist and I could get on with some of them. Never really being part of society, I was realising that I had mostly judged the rest of society's values and norms on a standard based on my experience of being drunk and a social life existing in drink world. Yet, all worlds have their particular rules and etiquette and at one time I applied the custom of asking someone to have one yourself, a line offered to a member of the bar staff or to a person that one might be drinking with, outside the confines of a pub. It is a common practice but, like a lot of things, they become bizarre if the same words and meaning are applied in another social setting.

I tried out this theory of mine in a cake shop near where I live. It was an old fashioned shop. The lady served me my apple danish or whatever and I said, "Have one yourself." I then went on to offer a round to the other elderly ladies in the shop. "What's your poison, a macaroon, Chelsea bun, or chocolate éclair ? Go on, I can stretch to real fresh cream." And so it went but, after trying out this idea a few times and not having any takers except for the odd stare from some, I stopped my new line in social gracing.

Still, a proper job came my way. An old friend, Dave, told me to go for this job working on a 'one to one' with people with severe learning disabilities. It meant working for the National Health Service. I was told that the disabled people that I would be with are hard to work with and they were labelled as having challenging behaviour. My job was to develop a relationship with them. I did that type of work for years. I didn't see it as a proper job. I often enjoyed taking someone to look at trains, having an ice cream or going for a drive, just a disabled person and me, a person who found it difficult to be around others and others found it difficult to be around him or her. It seemed to fit. The staff are the problem, of course.

A few years back, a bit of my 'Lurker' past came back to me. One morning, before going into my job, I had a phone call from 'Ginger Productions'. It is or maybe was a company owned by the entrepreneurial DJ Chris Evans, asking if I had The Lurker's LP's. On the television show 'Don't Forget Your Toothbrush', they were going to have the footballer Stuart Pearce on their show. I was told that Stuart was an old fan of the group. This I knew as I had been told and read it before. They told me Beggar's Banquet had given them my number. Now, I was never one for hobnobbing but Pete Edwards (Plug) our old roadie had arranged it all, so off we went one Friday afternoon to the recording of the show. It was interesting watching the 'wanna be' people race around. Anyway, they didn't use the item of Stuart the punk but told me that Stuart was back stage and would I like to say 'Hello', so to speak. He was with his wife and an old friend of his. I was struck by how very ordinary he was in his dress and presence. He seemed to be a very nice chap and appeared delighted to talk about The Lurkers and what the other members of the group were doing. He remained a fan and pointed out to me on the back of one of the LP covers where he is in the crowd as a fifteen year old lad with his mates. Judging by the expression on his wife's face, I would say she had heard enough about Stuart's punk days over the years.

Now, Pete (Plug) is a big football fan and was really pleased about having a chat with Stuart Pearce however, what struck me was that Stuart was still a fan of punk music. He had good look at me, he seemed pleased and called me 'Manic', my name in The Lurkers being Manic Esso. Being a stupid sod and master of the obvious, I tapped him on his shoulder and said, "Well, you got into football then ?" "Yes Manic," he said. "You've done well at it though," I went on. "Thanks Manic," he said politely. He must have thought, 'this 'Manic' might have played drums but he's a bit thick'. I thought about it afterwards. The bloke was Captain of the English football team and I remind him that he has got an involvement with football. Still, it was pleasant to meet him. We shook hands and then Pete (Plug) and me got on the Central Line and went to the pub for a drink.

Talking of football, I know this chap Mark Wyeth who is a Chelsea fanatic. He works as a Barrister but his other personality is to be a punk singer. He is a friend of Paul Fox, the guitarist with The Ruts. Mark asked me to drum on a retro 7 inch blue vinyl record in 1997 when Chelsea got to the Cup Final. The group was called The Chelsea Punk All Stars. It was a coincidence playing with Paul, what with him doing the recording with Pete and me in 1985 or 86. It was sold to help a charity. Mark later asked me to be involved in a scene he's got going called Club Ska but I'm too much of a miserable sod I suppose.

People at work take holidays. I visit people I know for my break. A few years back I bumped into this bloke in a local pub whom I didn't really know but had seen him around my area years ago. He has been living in California donkey's years and I should have had my suspicions as he wore baseball hats and enjoyed his American mouth wash accent. To cut it short, he invited me to stay at his place with his wife and child. Me being a bit of an opportunist and a useless judge of character took him up on his offer. He painted a rosy picture of all things American but he, like many others in that society have their facts fucked with fiction. On my first night, I knew it was bad, him telling me that Tom Hanks is like the second coming for opening up people's eyes to suffering and what's going on the world. He had me down as a cynic within sixteen hours of touch down Stateside. It was all bollocks. I lasted two nights.

I didn't know the bloke so I shouldn't have gone there. He lived seventy five miles south of San Francisco. The Beat invasion of the fifties with the likes of Jack Kerouac has given the place a name but the psyche of surf, sun and being chilled is a shallow veneer to a spiteful culture. Just south from there is John Steinbeck country. I went to where he came from but couldn't evoke any meaningful feelings; it was a shame. I stayed with this bloke's brother-in-law for a night. His father was a minister but what holds sway is all things first, then a bit of spiritual reflection for afters. On sighting an old chap down on his luck, I remarked how incongruous he appeared as we were in a middle class area, what with the sun and gleaming cars and neat gardens. He couldn't understand what I meant and kept referring to this man, as many Americans do as a Bum. "We've got lots of bums out here," he said. I told him that the man was not a bum and it's a word that I didn't think aptly describes someone's economic and emotional downfall. I wasn't being overly pious, it was just the fucking attitude was pissing me off. He still couldn't understand, saying, "Well I guess the guy made too many negative decisions in his life." I asked him where he had read that in the Bible, what with him being a believer and his dad being a Minister. In what story could I find those words of compassion, in the adventures of old Jesus and the other dropouts on the edge of society, when exactly did He make that value judgement as he walked down the avenue of a thousand sandals ?

After this incident I still had nearly two weeks before the holiday was over and when I now look back it was like a boring February afternoon waiting for a bus or train to get home and having flu. I got on a train and went to Reno; nice scenery and a nice train in a society where paranoia is as natural as breathing. The spirit of the Wild West is evident as fear and suspicion of the stranger threads itself through the very fabric of daily life. A bloke travelling with his father spoke to me on the train after I initiated conversation. He later met me when I was talking to the woman who worked behind the counter in the refreshment car. She told me of her plans of going to Paris. She came from Chicago. We talked about politics and people. This bloke listened for a while before going off and returning with a camera. He asked if we minded him taking a photo of us. I didn't, she didn't and so he took some photographs and then went off. She told me that he was interested because she was black and I was white, she went on to tell me that was the way it is, "White liberals". She told me that I wouldn't like that part of the world. I saw the man again when getting off the train at Reno. I went to shake his hand but he warned me against it, telling me not to shake hands with people as it was the quickest way to catch flu. I was in Reno. A few days later I got a bus back to San Francisco to wait the week before my plane left.

From the people whom I encountered, it was usually the black people I found to be the most friendly and had any wit about them in sharing a joke or of being conscious of what's going on. Although, any conversations I had in the land of the free was of the fleeting transitory sort. I got a room on the edge of the Chinese quarter in San Francisco and spent the week gazing at this duped and hyped place. For example, they must have filmed the television series The Streets Of San Francisco in about three streets and I found about four bars in an area described as being a 'labyrinth of rock and blues bars' and so it went on.

There seemed to be an inordinate amount of homeless people who were primarily made up of mentally ill and black people. Whilst I was one of my walks one day, I was mooching along a barren area of the harbour, I bumped into this chap. I heard this 'clip clop' sound and on turning saw this man using a paddling style with his feet to propel his body that was in an old pram. His arms and upper body appeared useless. He told me that he was in his fifties but had forgotten exactly. He used to work in a warehouse across the water in Oakland, in the days when he had his health, wife and kids. His health failed, his wife and family didn't want to know him and the "blacks, queers, sexually perverted, Jewish and mugging scum" ruined it all for everyone. At first I went to give him a dollar but he waved it aside telling me that he didn't beg. I walked with him for about a mile. I watched his technique of moving his pram *cum* wheelchair, the long plodding pulls as the heels of his worn trainers hit the ground. He told me that he had use of his arms but his method used less effort. The sum total of this man's life was packed in a precise and ordered way into a few disposable bags on the back of his vehicle. 'There it is,' I thought, all of his secrets and private belongings. His manner was abrupt as he asked me if I knew what Dover in England was like. He told me that he had read about it in a book, it was a detective story. He said it sounded interesting, what with the fog, the sea and the ships and that he wanted to go there sometime. I looked across at the sun crested view of the harbour spreading out to the sea and imagined it on a winter's evening with a drifting fog and ships barely visible. He told me that he had nothing to do with welfare, preferring to sleep in doorways, taking his chances there rather than sharing a room in a hostel with "the fag, transsexual, drug crazed, aids-ridden niggers". Across the main road I watched the office workers going for a jog. It looked like an arduous routine, an addition to their day's work, in their shorts and vests of gaudy bright colours, the reward being sun tanned bodies signifying a vitality that placed them as winners in a game.

One early evening whilst in this bar that was in an arty area, I listened to a bloke talking to a young barman. The barman was a student of this other bloke who spoke in a conceited tone of matters academic and intellectual. I half joined their chat, wanting to talk to him about John Steinbeck as this bloke was a literature lecturer. Anyway, to cut it short, the bloke had no time for people who fell in our society and at that point the door opened and the mad staring face of a young black girl, no older than thirteen, asked through broken teeth and a smile, "What can I get with a dollar ?" The barman shouted, "Out" at her, as if she was an unwanted mad dog vomiting rabid bile at his children. The girl's face left the scene. I reminded this wanker that she happened to be mentally ill, most probably homeless and he should count his blessings for the small mercy that had graced him with his brain, even though it was good only for a door stop. He went on to echo the American stanza on rugged individualism, saying everyone has choices and the "that wouldn't be me" speech. I offered to the bloke that some things are out of our control, telling him that someone just like him has been hit by a car today whilst crossing the road. There was no choice in the matter. You have no say in it, a lump of steel did it and it doesn't make a value judgement. The tosser of a lecturer bloke chipped in, "We have too much of that scum here," he said, referring to the young girl. I told him John Steinbeck was wasted on him; then I lost my temper, told him his fortune in a way that he deserved to be told and threatened to whack him for being such a nasty bastard.

I left the bar, not wanting to get nicked for hitting someone. Compassion was in short supply in this town. The bar was on a junction called Jack Kerouac Street. It looked like a fucking library from the outside. I looked around myself at the names of the artists and writers; given to what ? I had no feeling of interest. It was all just a pose, pretentious consumerist shit. I was thinking of the people that I had met and it all crashed in. The place seemed to be infested with black mentally ill people as if they were there for the winners, those functional to the machine, to judge themselves by in a paranoiac cesspool. I don't know if it was because of loneliness but I saw people as an appendage; nowhere near as valued as the method and all that it encompasses with its psyche of the immediate, oscillating uneasily with a soul that can't ever be quenched by trinkets.

A couple of years later I saw a programme on television about punk. Johnny Rotten spoke of his first visit to the United States of America and of how the place excited him. He still lives there. Well, I've never met the bloke but I thought about my last visit and my experience of the American way. I found it to be a robotised place with a language of swapping labels, designer speech and behaviour. You can't go for a walk; you have to be 'A Walker'. Everything is to be harnessed. The individual seems to be a figment of the American imagination. It wouldn't surprise me if very soon the middle classes are required to send formal letters if they wish to engage in social contact with guidelines of acceptable subjects to be discussed, sent by their lawyers for them to socialise appropriately when in public places; the type is all.

And yet, it's a shame, not forgetting the influence American groups had on me. My favourite writers come from there with great actors in films depicting the importance of a person whatever status that person might have. It can be through the small person that the larger emotions and significant meanings to us all are incorporated. The small person is not patronised as is the case in the UK where just accent and social position depicts the complexity of a person's worth and their relationship to the world. As I say, it's a shame. Maybe it was just that it was California, I don't know.

'To be a punk'.

To know the philosophy of difference. Some say it is rebelling but it is to know and feel inside the non-content yet having idealism to what could be. It is not rallying a call to arms because there is no change in sight and maybe the marginal men have always had their role to play in giving others insight to themselves. It has nothing to do with what sex, race, class, age or whatever a person might be. Through my experiences, it feels to me, that the punk thing gave me my identity. From my experience in Ireland for example, when looking at inequity and the politics that deal with people who are being excluded, I found that many of the people there who were fighting the system to have the same traits of following fashion, language and yearning for conventional trappings and a self interest for personal gain in a system that they decry. I felt the outsider within as I learned that if the politics of difference was taken out of it, many people that I had met shared the same cultural references and aspirations for things and values as those I felt I had nothing in common with in the place that I come from. So, it was just the bracketing of that difference where I shared a common ground. I realised that I didn't share other social references, it was, is, yet another team.

The punk thing continues to offend. If at work when talking about music to an old blues-rock musician, I find they get a bit shirty. It is now years after the punk thing had made its entry to the mainstream but there are many that will not forget and in their resentful way, forgive what they saw as a personal intrusion into their little world. One occasion, only a few years ago, when asked to play with a local group, this boring sod spotted The Lurkers written on my drum case when we were having a rehearsal. This put him off, offending his provincial sensitivities. He snided on behind my back about being a musician. He imagined that he was a session man for Bob Seger or someone. I'll say it again; people like him wear the tired cynicism of being on the road when they've only been down the road.

The Lurkers' ability to be 'un hip' continues. We are nearly always left out of punk compilations and that kind of thing even though we sold quite a few for being a cult group. It made me smile to read in a magazine a while ago an article by the journalist Julie Burchill. She was going on about how she never liked the punk thing and of how she preferred to listen to soul music but had to suffer groups like The Lurkers and The Drones; all white, male, anti sex and love and of how she couldn't wait to get home and listen to Barry White or The Isley Brothers. Leigh Heggarty, a chap with an encyclopaedic knowledge of pop music, showed this article to me. He told me that she came from Brighton or Bristol and used punk to further her career. Exactly, she should have stayed in Brighton or Bristol or wherever it was that she came from. Making a living out of things and people that you don't particularly like is one thing but taking the piss as well is taking liberties. People such as her in the media world with its superficial creations that she and her type inhabit, have a quality of being insincere and are parasitical but have always been around, so why would a thing like The Lurkers appeal or the feel and philosophy of difference ?

A couple of years back, Banquet Records Ltd had a party. It was a glittery, coming of age affair and we were invited. Pete Edwards (Plug) still works for them so I suppose it was his idea to ask us. Well, Nigel and myself went but Pete (Stride) didn't. It was corporate. There were chill rooms with toys and games for tall children with beaky faces, glasses, gelled hair and satchels on their backs. They looked like evacuees from some kind of inter planetary war. Martin Mills didn't even recognise Nigel. It was a long way from that rehearsal room in Fulham. I thought about Beggar's at that time, not knowing a lot about music but being in the right place at the right time and here they are now, minus Nick Austin, the company had done well. Mike Stone was there. He told me that he was doing his own thing up in the Midlands. I thought through the years, it all felt the same. A feeling of loneliness, fear, a fractured self with no strong identity. I listened to mockney accents. Mike asked why I wasn't pissed. "You mad bastard," he said. I thought about it, maybe six or seven days in twenty eight years I had gone without a drink and I thought about my moods. I shift from raising the roof to wanting to swing from it. Mike always had me pigeon holed as mad bastard.

The feeling of difference has been compounded by the attitude of others with their classification. I thought of Pete (Stride), Nigel and me and I thought of our solitariness, of being anxious and of being left out of *normal* situations and I thought of what has been learned from therapy and of all the mysteries and the craving. I stood back and looked around myself. It felt lonely. Anyway, I know sod all about the music scene and never have. The 'muso biz' thing left me cold but I did go and see Screaming Lord Sutch play in a local pub, to me not that long before he died. He was doing his show that he had done for years. I tried to talk to him, I wanted to say 'hello' and tell him that I played in a group and that our first gig was with him and that he must have thought we were a green bunch. I wanted to say thanks to him for being a nice bloke who had understanding but it was too late, he had gone mad. It was not an act for him as he went through in mechanical fashion his public routine of giving people false money and repeating with eyes that never strayed from a place thirty yards or metres in front of himself, "We're the only party that give away money." He was lost. You couldn't reach him if you borrowed a space probe from NASA. I stood to the side and felt saddened.

Not long after that evening he was dead. A depressed man, alone in his room, he hung himself. It must have been grim for him when thinking of those boring sods that attached themselves to his party; all those 'raving loonies'. The torment in the end of mixing with reactionary types who run country pubs, who make sarcastic quips and who have an officially approved set of jokes. It must have depressed Dave to hell when being invited to one of their events and feeling that he had to through the routine for the wives and bearing up to yet another night of loony behaviour by accountants shaving half their beards off and doing Monty Python silly walks but always to retain a very Englishness and that, for them, usually means being a bigoted wanker who is the 'naughty but nice' man who is crazy but clean and has objectives of being invited around the house of some rural MP and, when there, starts fawning around for the amusement of the MP's children.

It must have been grim to share the last years with these types. To sit at their dinner table and when the jokes are finished, the official raving loon loosens a scout sock from his neck and becomes serious, maybe saying things like, "but if I want to eat smoked vole sandwiches I will, my family have for years." Well, that kind of thing.

Yes, Dave must have looked at their odd sock wearing, bow tie spinning behaviour and felt alone. I pondered over entertainment, the people involved and its function. The clowns who want crowns; those that are accepted and are commissioned to be revolting for regality. Those subjects who have a stylised behaviour that conforms, from media figures to those from the comedy industry telling jokes to make the little Royal laugh and the crazy, rock 'n' rollers dressed up in their pantomime outfits, playing loud music for the powerful people who live in big castles and are big in land owning and arms dealing and their agents would kill each other so that their client gets the charity gig. I had thoughts of Muhammed Ali, 'the greatest', and those who live and have lived and are known and are not known, those that stand to one side and hold a mirror up to the rest in society. It gets as lonely as Benny Hill and then, I stopped pondering.

It was put to me that I ought to tell my tale by Mark Wyeth and Leigh Heggarty. Leigh showed me the book that DJ Steve Lamacq had out called 'Going Deaf for a Living'. In the book he talked of his liking of The Lurkers. It was shown to me to point out that there are people, some, who would be interested in reading a 'Lurker' story. It is said that everyone has a story to tell, so I've told mine. It's a way of addressing and coming to terms with the punk thing; to enjoy and remember its value, not to harp on about but to realise.

Working with people who have severe learning disabilities and are mentally ill is okay. As I've said my issue has been with the *normals*. My personality hasn't been that accepted by many of those *normals* at work but fuck them, even though at times they have increased my anxiety and I learned that a lot of my paranoia is justified. I had started writing the story when one morning I walked though the security door of a large Day Centre and a chap that I will call Jack who has a learning disability came rushing up to me. His face was four inches from my mine as he said excitedly, "Guess what Pete ? Joey Ramone has died." I told him that I didn't know he had heard of The Ramones and he went on to sing some lines of their songs. I didn't know Jack that well but he had heard that I once played in a punk group. He told me 'Sheena Is A Punk Rocker' was his favourite. I looked at a member of staff who came and stood next to Jack, an unfortunate type who is in that work for purposes to control but his inadequacies didn't end there. "That's good," I remarked to him about Jack being a Ramones fan. The member of staff raised his eyebrows. I knew punk had intruded into this person's musical world. "I don't think so," he said in that unoriginal Friends accent and tone. He then nodded to a photograph of Rick Wakeman that he had on the wall of his room. "That's the man," he said. Exactly. I told Jack that we'd get a gun and go out and get all the boring bastards that have pissed us off.

My mind went back to the night we played in Leicester with the blind man in his wheel chair, staring forward through small black glasses but not seeing. His silhouette spread against the wall behind him, an expression of pleasure but his face in a kind of grimace. There he was alone. The image sent a chill down my back. I looked at Jack. Words came to me, 'My heart's in the shadow'. To be away from the others, the grabbing, punching, craving, competing and away from the noise, aside, offstage.

It's quiet here, with God's Lonely Men.